Russian Literary Profiles No. 1

LEONID ANDREYEV

Josephine M. Newcombe
University of Bristol

BRADDA BOOKS LTD
Letchworth, Hertfordshire, England
1972

Copyright © 1972 Josephine M. Newcombe

Printed in Belgium by Jos Adam, Brussels

Chapter I

Early years

In the first decade of the present century Leonid Andreyev was regarded as one of the most talented writers in Russia. Each new story or play he wrote was eagerly discussed by literary critics and bought in record numbers by a large reading public. Andreyev even looked like the popular image of a writer with his flowing dark hair, pale complexion, expressive eyes and unconventional clothes. By 1908 he had earned enough money to build himself a large house in Finland in which he lived in a fairly extravagant style, although the luxury of his way of life was always exaggerated by gossip writers. Then gradually his reputation dwindled, although Andreyev continued to write prolifically, and first the critics and then his readers deserted him. After the October revolution of 1917 Andreyev lived in near poverty until his death two years later. His swift rise to fame and equally swift decline can be partly explained by the fact that his writings were very much a reflection of the mood of the early twentieth century and the impact of new ideas in Russia. Once the first world war and revolutions had destroyed this mood for ever, then Andreyev's works had lost much of their force. Despite this, his considerable output of stories and plays undoubtedly contains much talented writing, and is of interest to the modern reader.

Leonid Andreyev was born on 21st August 1871 in Orel, a provincial capital of about 60,000 inhabitants some 200 miles to the south of Moscow. His parents were both natives of Orel, and had few advantages of wealth or education. Nikolai Andreyev, Leonid's father, was the illegitimate son of a landowner and a peasant girl, and was given something of a start in life by three years of secondary education and rudimentary professional training. After this he was able to get a low paid post as a land-tax assessor, working for the railway company. In 1870 Nikolai fell in love with and married a local girl, Anastasiya Patskovskaya. His income was then only 15 roubles a month, but after the birth of his first child Leonid, he managed to get a better job in one of the town banks, and now had enough money to build his own house. The house was one storey high, and built of wood, and there was enough land for a garden and orchard at the back. The street where Leonid was to live until the age of twenty was on the outskirts of the town, near the river Orlik, in the same rough area where his father had himself grown up. Most of the people who lived there were very poor artisans, and their only recreation was drinking and fighting in the streets. The atmosphere in the poorer districts of Orel was probably not unlike that of Nizhni Novgorod in the same decade, which Maxim Gorky described in his novel *Childhood*. Nikolai Andreyev was respected by his neighbours because he earned more money than they did, and for his great physical strength and prowess in fights. He was a man of strong character, and his wife and children accepted his authority, but he was not brutal, and the cruel beatings which Gorky experienced as a child were never a feature of the Andreyev household. Leonid's mother had been left an orphan at the age of 10, and could hardly read and write, but she had a lively imagination and enjoyed telling stories to her children. Anastasiya Andreyev was very fond of her eldest son, and none of the five children born later, three boys and two girls, were ever to be as dear to her. Leonid returned this love, and throughout his whole life spent only very brief periods away from his mother. She moved to Moscow to be near him when he entered the university, and formed part of his household during his two marriages. The strong bond between them was reinforced when she was widowed, and Leonid at the age of 17 accepted responsibility as head of the family.

The Andreyevs lived modestly but had enough money to avoid any real hardship, and Leonid's childhood was reasonably carefree. He was an active boy, and spent as much time as he could exploring the countryside round Orel, and in winter liked to skate along the river. He got on well with other boys in the street, fought and played with them, and led them in games, which he often invented himself. Nikolai Andreyev got up at six every morning, and expected everyone else in the family to do the same, so Leonid had long days free to do more or less what he pleased in the years before he went to grammar school. His father spent a lot of time working in the garden in the months when there was no snow on the ground, and Leonid was also a passionate gardener in later life, trying hard to cultivate the poor soil of his Finnish home. A more harmful habit passed on from father to son was heavy drinking. Nikolai Andreyev would invite his friends to join him for an evening's drinking at home, and they would get through vast quantities of vodka and beer, usually leading to noisy scenes and fights. Leonid was never able to overcome the tendency to indulge in prolonged drinking bouts, sometimes for two or three days on end, particularly when he was depressed. Nikolai liked his son, and Leonid never criticised him in later life, but it was his mother who really encouraged the boy to develop the artistic side of his personality. She came from an impoverished landowning family, who in their more prosperous days had boasted some talented members, artistically and musically gifted. Leonid had learnt to read at home by the age of six. At seven he was given a subscription to a local lending library, and he read avidly more or less anything he could get hold of. His mother passed on a fondness for adventure stories, the more fantastic the better, and Leonid's favourite authors for many years were Jules Verne, Mayne Reid, and Fenimore Cooper. As he grew older he came to enjoy Poe's *Tales of Mystery and Imagination* and Dickens' novels, and these two writers clearly influenced his own fiction. To get some peace from his brothers and sisters he would climb on to the roof of the house and settle down to read for hours on end. It was Leonid's mother who first took him to the local theatre, and this also captured the boy's imagination and led to his lifelong interest in drama. Leonid soon showed a natural aptitude for drawing and painting, and at one time even thought of becoming a professional artist. He did good portraits of his friends, but preferred painting fantastic pictures out of his head. Demons, devils and grotesque faces fascinated him for a long time, and this preference for imaginary subjects was later to be true of his

9

writing, where he chose historical or fantastic settings for many stories and plays. Painting remained one of his favourite hobbies all his life.

In September 1882 Leonid entered Class 1 of the Orel grammar school, and life became a more serious matter. The school buildings were dark and gloomy and looked like a military barracks. The teachers as employees of the state wore uniform frock coats, and were formal and distant from the boys whom they taught. The education Leonid received from his eleventh year was standard throughout Russia, and by far the greater part of the time was spent learning Greek and Latin. Science was not taught, and Russian literature was only studied up to 1850, according to new regulations introduced in 1871. The notoriously reactionary Minister of Education, Count Dmitri Tolstoy, believed that the study of classical languages and mathematics disciplined the mind, whereas science and history were potentially dangerous to the state because they encouraged pupils to ask questions. School life with its harsh discipline and uninspiring teaching was a great contrast to the freedom Leonid had enjoyed at home, and while he received good marks in his first couple of years in the school, as he grew into adolescence he began to rebel. He broke rules where he could, smoked, refused to get his hair cut and drew caricatures of the teachers. Later in life Andreyev described his school as a place where originality and talent were stifled, and the teachers as pedantic and uninteresting. The headmaster made frequent use of the birch and detention to punish boys, and taught Russian literature according to stereotyped theories. The boys had to write essays according to a strict formula which left little scope for the imagination, or translate passages from Greek keeping as close to the original text as possible. Leonid's best subject was Russian composition, and he eventually developed a plan to cut down the amount of time spent on homework, on which he resented wasting his evenings. He used to arrive early at school and dash off about five or six essays on the same subject for his friends. In return they helped him with his classics and mathematics in which he was weaker. By the time he got to the end of his sixth year in school he was getting such poor marks that he was not allowed to take the examinations for entry into Class 7. Later he recalled that summer in an article written when he was a reporter for a Moscow paper. While all his friends studied hard for the exams, painfully learning irregular verbs, Leonid went for long walks in the country, strolled along river banks, lay in the long grass, talked to peasants in the fields and 'wrote bad verse'.

After some years at grammar school Leonid was no longer the happy boy he had been at eleven. He spent more and more time on his own, although he was respected and liked by his classmates, because of his fearless defiance of authority, and his good looks. Leonid had grown into a handsome youth, and conscious that people were staring at him, he developed a manner of looking straight ahead when walking. As he grew older he began to experience the moods of extreme depression which were to affect him from time to time throughout his life. His reading now became more serious, and one of the books which affected him deeply was Tolstoy's *What I Believe*. This had been written in 1884, and then banned for publication by the government of Alexander III because of Tolstoy's pacifist views and attacks on nearly every kind of state institution and the Orthodox church. The book circulated in clandestine copies, which must have made it all the more interesting to schoolboys living in the 1880s, a decade unmatched for the severity of the censorship and power of the autocracy over every part of people's lives. Leonid also read Russian translations of Schopenhauer's *The World as Will and Idea* and Hartmann's *Philosophy of the Unconscious*, and both writers were to have some influence on his later ideas about the world. These pessimistic philosophers were

12

popular among the Russian intellectuals of the 1880s, many of whom despaired of seeing any reform of the autocratic system in Russia.

At the age of sixteen Leonid felt sufficiently disillusioned by life to try to commit suicide. Returning from a party with a group of friends one evening, he fell behind the crowd who were laughing and enjoying themselves. Walking along beside the railway line he suddenly felt that life had no purpose, and remembered his reading of Tolstoy. Leonid couldn't believe in God, yet accepted Tolstoy's view that all social institutions were corrupt, and felt that there was no point in living. He lay down between the rails as a train approached to see whether 'providence' wanted him to live. The train passed over him and tore his jacket, but left Leonid unharmed. After this episode he felt a sense of relief, but his depression soon returned, and he was near to suicide again several times.

The idea of becoming a writer had occurred to Andreyev by the time he was seventeen. In an entry in his diary he resolved to become a 'famous writer,' and wrote that he intended to destroy established moral codes. He spent some time working on technique, first improving the prose of his diary entries, and then trying to imitate the style of many different writers.

In 1889 Nikolai Andreyev died suddenly from a brain haemorrhage. Leonid was now nearly eighteen years old, repeating a year in Class 6 at school, and in a rebellious self-preoccupied mood. Andreyev's short story *In Springtime* (1900) recalls this mood. The young hero of the story, Pavel, is contemplating suicide, and feels that he cannot communicate with his family, when the unexpected news of his father's death makes him realise that he has a duty to look after his mother and her other children. Pavel experiences a new wish to live and a sense of purpose, much as Leonid must have done. Serious financial problems affected the family after Nikolai Andreyev's death, and it was to be more than ten years before they escaped from poverty. There were no savings or other source of income for the family of six children, so Leonid tried to help his mother by giving lessons, doing statistical work for a local government office, and spending nights on end painting pictures of military uniforms. He earned very little from these activities, yet his mother never suggested that he should leave school. The Andreyevs learned to make use of any charities which were available, and Leonid was exempted from paying fees in his last two years at school.

The poor marks which Leonid received in Class 7, where he was in bottom place all year, were partly due to the amount of time he spent trying to earn money, but also the result of an emotional disturbance. He had fallen very passionately in love with a girl of his own age called Zinaida. Leonid's good looks do not seem to have impressed Zinaida, although most of the other schoolgirls of the town were infatuated with him, and Leonid tormented himself because she did not return his love. In the final year at school he did make an effort to put her out of his mind, and was able to get some work done, passed the exams and was awarded the school leaving certificate necessary for entry to university.

Leonid's mother was determined that he should enter university despite the appalling financial strain it would put on the family. She mortgaged their house and small piece of land, and Leonid enrolled in the law faculty of St. Petersburg University in August 1891. It may seem strange that he chose to become a lawyer, since this had never been one of his ambitions as a boy, but no fewer than eleven of his classmates decided on the same subject, and he may well have preferred to go to a new and strange environment with them. He chose to go to St. Petersburg rather than Moscow which was 400 miles nearer home, because Zinaida was already studying there. Life in the capital must have been a challenging experience for Andreyev, who until then had never been far from his native Orel. Shortage of money meant that he lived in uncomfortable cheap lodgings, and for the first time in his life often had to go hungry. He tried to make extra money, but without much success at first, and a story he wrote about a starving student was rejected by the magazine he sent it to. Leonid did not settle in to university life, and felt depressed and dissatisfied with himself, because of lack of progress in his studies. He was still hopelessly attracted to Zinaida, and could not overcome this passion although it conflicted with the high ideals he set himself. One disturbing incident during his first year at university was a reminder of the restrictive society he lived in. His mother was arrested in Orel because she had rented a room to a man wanted by the police, although she in fact knew nothing about him. For this minor infringement of the law Mrs. Andreyev was sent to prison in Moscow, and later transferred to St. Petersburg. During her month on remand there, Leonid visited his mother in prison and petitioned for her release, and she was eventually able to return home.

In the autumn of 1892 Leonid came back for his second year at university. Shortly afterwards Zinaida announced that she was getting married to an engineer, and Leonid was so depressed by the news that he tried to stab himself with a dagger after a party. Fortunately he did not do any serious damage to himself, but he felt unable to stay in St. Petersburg, and went home to Orel for good in November. The following June the university asked him to leave because he had not paid his fees. At home Leonid recovered a little from his depression, although he was drinking heavily and began to worry that he might be a hereditary alcoholic. Eventually he decided to enter the law faculty of Moscow university, and applied for financial help to both the town of Orel and the Moscow Committee of the 'Society for Aid to Needy Students'. The society after some delay agreed to pay his fees. (In his story *The Grand Slam* Andreyev makes one of his characters pay regular contributions to this fund, perhaps as a tribute to the help it gave him.)

In Moscow, too, Leonid was unhappy away from his family, whose support he apparently needed. All his life he liked to be surrounded by near relatives and friends. In January 1894 after four months away from home, deeply depressed by another unsuccessful love affair, he made two more suicide attempts. He began to drink heavily again, but by the summer of 1894 he was back to some equilibrium, and passed the mid-course exams. The problem of getting enough money to live on still preoccupied his family, and in 1895 Mrs. Andreyev decided to sell off the mortgaged Orel house and move with the whole family to Moscow. After the meagre proceeds of the sale had been spent the only regular income for the family was the second son Vsevolod's wage of 15 roubles a month, earned in a government office. Leonid spent hours walking round Moscow trying to find tutoring work which could bring in a little money. The Andreyevs lived in a series of dilapidated small flats in Moscow, often in damp basements. There was little money left after the rent had been paid, and often the children had to go hungry. They pawned any valuables they had, sold their best clothes, and one of the sisters earned thirty kopecks a day in a corset factory. Leonid's efforts were rewarded by the end of 1895, when he managed to get an article and two stories published in the *Orel Herald*. The subject matter shows his preoccupations at this time, for the article attacked the meanness of the public who didn't contribute to students' charities, and pointed out the sufferings of badly-off students. Later he was able to earn more money composing advertisements in newspaper offices. Conditions might be hard but at least Leonid could now live with his own family rather than in student lodgings, and his mother was able to soothe him on days when he felt very depressed. She never lost faith in his capabilities, and was sure that he would eventually lead the family out of poverty. It is remarkable how similar was the pattern of Andreyev's life at this time to that of Anton Chekhov, who a decade earlier had studied at Moscow university, and tried to keep a family of similar size once his father was no longer capable of earning. Despite financial worries Leonid's letters of this period, when the family were reunited, are full of jokes and a new enjoyment of life. Vodka was cheap, and Leonid still drank heavily in common with most of the poorer students of that time, who could not afford any other kind of recreation. Lack of money does not seem to have prevented Leonid from visiting the theatre frequently and he saw most interesting new productions. Andreyev's two plays *The Days of Our Life* and *Gaudeamus* recreate the atmosphere of student life in the 1890s, with its superficial cheerfulness concealing many social problems.

The acceptance of his stories by the *Orel Herald* was a great stimulus to Andreyev to write more, and he finished several in 1896-7, but none were accepted. Evidently the editors didn't appreciate Andreyev's imitation of fashionable 'modernistic' trends in his prose. Leonid could have sat for his final law exams in 1896 but he felt unprepared, as his efforts to earn money had left him little time for studying and the exams were to be held a month earlier because of the coronation of the new tsar,

Nicholas II. Leonid didn't go to the celebrations, at which a fatal stampede occurred resulting in the death of over a thousand people, because his shoes were in such a bad state; but later that day he saw some of the bodies brought back, and probably shared the indignation of many Russians that the royal couple attended a ball that evening. Another more personal event in Leonid's life in the summer of 1896 was his first meeting with his future wife, Alexandra Veligorskaya. Alexandra was also from Orel, and the couple met by chance in a village not far from Moscow where Leonid was giving some lessons. In April 1897 after feverish revision he took his final exams and passed fairly well, gaining the equivalent of a second class degree. He was happy at his success, and wrote in his diary, 'I want to live, to shake off the dirt, boredom and vodka of student days, and to work.' He was offered a post in the Ministry of Justice but decided to enter private legal practice, where the income was less secure but the restrictions not quite so great. Andreyev soon discovered that speaking in court made him extremely nervous, and although he was successful in his first three cases he was not reassured by this. In fact his legal career was to be short-lived. As fees received by junior lawyers were very small, and the Andreyev family finances had not improved, it was still necessary for Leonid to look for extra work. By a lucky chance, he was offered something which was much better suited to his temperament and abilities than the formalities of the courts. He began to write reports of court cases for a paper called the *Moscow Herald*. Andreyev's reports were well received, and he was soon offered the post of a permanent contributor. Now he was able to write articles on general topics as well as legal ones, and more important for his future career, he also began to place reports in a newly established paper called *The Courier*.

Chapter II

Maxim Gorky
and the 'Wednesday Circle'

Andreyev achieved his early ambition of becoming a famous writer much more quickly than he could have dreamt possible. By 1903 nearly all the leading writers and critics in Russia had said something in public about Andreyev, and he enjoyed the reputation of being one of the most promising young writers. He was certainly helped by a series of lucky chances, but it was by the quality of his own writing that he made his name. Association with *The Courier* was the first major piece of luck for Andreyev. This paper had been founded in November 1897 by a group of young writers who intended it to be a fairly progressive paper with high literary standards, and at various times most of the well known writers of the day contributed, including Chekhov, Gorky and Bunin. Reporting was of a high standard, and controversial political subjects were not avoided, although articles were always liable to be censored. The four years Andreyev spent working as a journalist for *The Courier* was an invaluable period of literary apprenticeship, and later he said, 'There is no better school for an aspiring writer than to write to a deadline on a given topic.' Andreyev wrote court reports, satirical articles and reviews of books and plays, and also had twenty eight stories published in the magazine between 1898 and 1902. Journalism also gave Andreyev an opportunity to observe contemporary life carefully in order to find subjects for his articles. He cultivated a brisk style, aimed at holding the reader's attention, and something of this manner persisted in his stories. He now began to regard himself as a writer, and was as usual conscious of his good looks, referring to them facetiously in letters to friends in Orel: 'An abundant mane of dark hair frames my high forehead.' At last financial worries lessened as Andreyev could now earn up to 150 roubles a month, but he was developing more extravagant tastes and felt that this wasn't enough for life in Moscow. He took on as much work as he could, often spending up to 15 hours a day working, visiting law courts, writing and proof-reading in the newspaper offices. He was so exhausted after a year and a half of this life that the editorial board of *The Courier* paid for him to take a holiday on the Baltic coast.

Andreyev's journalism, apart from reports of court cases, consisted of observations on Moscow life. He adopted a pseudonym, James Lynch, and wrote under the headline, 'The Trifles of Life.' The subjects he wrote about were not always trivial, and he attacked many current social evils. Andreyev followed other writers, including Gorky, in complaining about the educated middle class, who were complacent and narrow-minded when so much needed to be done in Russia. In a typical article, *About the Russian Intellectual*, Andreyev considers over-devotion to rules and regulations to be one of the major vices of the middle class. 'The intellectual finds no time to work things out for himself, and in any case there's no need. A definite rule exists for every eventuality he's likely to meet.'

The first story Andreyev handed to the editors of *The Courier* was 'too confused and abstract' for their taste, so they advised him to pick a subject 'from real life' for the Easter number in 1898. Andreyev then wrote *Bargamot and Garaska*, a story which brought him to the attention of Maxim Gorky, (the pen name of Alexei Peshkov) and really launched his literary career. Gorky was three years older than Andreyev and had himself only been introduced to the Russian public in 1895, sponsored by the writer Korolenko, but was already highly successful. Perhaps because of his own early struggles against poverty he was always extraordinarily generous and helpful in encouraging and guiding new writers. In the spring of 1898 Gorky was in Nizhni Novgorod, and a local paper he subscribed to was suspended for three months. *The Courier* was sent out to readers instead. (It was another lucky chance that Andreyev's story was in the April number, for in May 1898 Gorky was arrested and taken by the police to Tiflis, where he spent some time in prison.) Gorky was sufficiently impressed by the story to write to the editor of *The Courier* to find out who Leonid Andreyev was. The action of *Bargamot and Garaska* takes place in the same street where Andreyev grew up in Orel, and the 'real life' which the editors recommended, with its descriptions of drinking and brawling, was not unlike the sort of life Gorky knew very well. It was this rather than the sentimentality of the story – a reconciliation at Easter between the local drunkard and a policeman—which impressed him.

Maxim Gorky influenced Andreyev's life profoundly. Despite later quarrels and their very different approach to life and literature they both continued to describe each other as 'my only true friend'. Gorky first met Andreyev very briefly at a railway station in Moscow, and recalling his first impressions he said, 'Andreyev was dressed in an old sheepskin coat with a

26

shaggy fur hat worn at an angle. He looked like a young actor from a Ukrainian troupe. He seemed very gay and excited.' Gorky was convinced that Andreyev was highly talented and personally encouraged him to accept the fact that he was a good writer, providing valuable introductions to editors and other writers. Gorky also gave Andreyev a lot of advice on how to write, which the younger man at first followed fairly carefully. At the beginning of 1900 Gorky introduced Andreyev to a group of writers known as the 'Wednesday Circle' the members of which met weekly and read out new works for mutual criticism. At his first visit Andreyev was too nervous and embarrassed to read out his story *Silence*, so Gorky read it for him. Teleshov, one of the writers who had founded the circle, was present at the meeting, and recalled the reading in his memoirs. Gorky introduced Andreyev 'who looked like a student, with a handsome face, very quiet, wearing a tobacco coloured jacket.' After the reading Mirolyubov, the editor of a popular magazine *Everybody's Journal*, went up to Andreyev, took the exercise book in which he had written the story, and put it in his pocket, much to Andreyev's pleasure. For the next four years Andreyev regularly attended meetings, and read out all his new stories, absorbing the criticism offered by the members.

The advice given to Andreyev by the editors of *The Courier* to write a story based on real life, and their rejection of his first attempt which seemed artificial to them, reflects the conflict at the turn of the century in the world of literature. The dominant mood of prose in Russia in the second half of the nineteenth century, critical realism, was challenged in the 1890s by a new generation of writers. French symbolist poetry became widely known and inspired a new Russian symbolist school. The symbolists, who broke with all past literary tradition, and called for a complete reassessment of poetry, shocked people by their daring, and were at first known as 'decadent writers'. There was considerable opposition to this new kind of writing, based on subtle shades of meanings, veiled allusions and a very wide range of vocabulary. In 1897, Leo Tolstoy, whose views still commanded enormous respect, wrote *What is Art*, a book attacking symbolist writing, which he said was obscure and could not be understood by the mass of the people. Tolstoy objected to the critics' praise of the new writers; 'And most of all note this, that the moment you admit that an art may be good which is unintelligible to any mentally sound people, there is not the slightest reason to hinder any little circle of corrupted people producing works which tickle their corrupted feelings, and are unintelligible to everyone except themselves, the very thing that is done now by the so-called decadents.' Despite such attacks the decadents flourished in the first decade of the century, writing both prose and poetry. At the same time many prose writers, still continuing the strong realist traditions of earlier years formed an opposing literary camp headed by Maxim Gorky. As Andreyev was helped so much by Gorky in the early days of his career, and as the members of the Wednesday circle were all realists, it was at first accepted that he would follow this path, but he was undoubtedly attracted by the new decadent writing, which seemed particularly in tune with the mood of the fin-de-siècle. It was fashionable to talk about mysticism and the 'unknown' surrounding human life. There was a general expectation that great changes would soon affect society, and a sense of impending catastrophe, and it was not long before Andreyev tried to express something of this mood in his fiction. In 1898 he published four stories, and 1899 saw twice that number, reflecting his increased confidence and improved technique. By 1900 his stories became much more ambitious in length and subject matter, and they were no longer merely imitative of Chekhov, Gorky and other writers, but reflected the first signs of what was to be Andreyev's own particular blend of realism and symbolism.

Andreyev's stories written between 1898 and 1902 show how he gradually moves away from a traditional manner. The first story which Andreyev had published outside *The Courier* was called *Peter at the Dacha* (*Everybody's Journal* September 1899) and is competently written rather in the style of Chekhov, although it is over sentimental. Peter is a ten year old boy who works long hours in a barber's shop in a poor area of the city. There is no future for Peter except a life of drinking, swearing, fighting and hunger, and the little boy seems dull and stupid, dumbly hoping that he may one day escape from his terrible surroundings. Then he is miraculously taken on a visit to the country, where contact with nature has an immediate healing effect. Peter, at first 'a town savage, uncertain how to behave in the country', soon learns to enjoy his freedom, running around in the fields and woods, but the inevitable tragedy happens, and he has to return to the barber's shop. The story is based on contrasts – the ugly town and beautiful countryside, disease and health, dull boredom and lively interest, restriction and freedom – perhaps a rather mechanical structure, but Peter's grief is well described and the reader's sympathy is aroused. Andreyev wrote several other stories of this type, in which children or defenceless adults are exploited by society. The description of the city as a place which is hostile to man, is a theme which was also to appear many times subsequently in Andreyev's fiction.

Two more ambitious stories of this time are *At the Window* (1899) and *On the River* (1900). The main character of *At the Window* is a clerk, Andrei Nikolayevich, whose work is to copy documents by hand. He has become terrified of real life, and only feels safe observing people from the window of his room. He has opportunities for promotion and marriage but is too frightened to accept because of the disturbance they will make in his life. This description of a poor clerk is hardly original in Russian literature, but there is a detail in the story which is one of Andreyev's constant themes. Andrei Nikolayevich, we are told, can shut himself up in his room, but he cannot escape his own thoughts, which literally tear down the walls he protects himself with. In later works Andreyev spends a lot of time discussing the destructive effect of thought on his heroes' lives. In *On the River*, a more optimistic story, an engineer, Aleksei Stepanovich, doesn't like his fellow human beings very much, and feels isolated in a community where he is not a native. Suddenly his life is changed by a spring flood which brings destruction to the area, but also gives Aleksei an opportunity to come into contact with people. In the hard work of rescuing his fellows, he discovers real happiness, and finds that he can get on with people. 'Until now he had not known that he liked people, and the sun, and he did not understand why they seemed different and why he wanted to laugh and cry ... It was as if he had discovered art for the first time, and the enjoyment of breathing'.

Andreyev's own memories of school and student days provide the raw material for a number of his stories, and these have more emotional impact because of the note of personal suffering. *The Festival* (1900), which has a seventeen year old boy as its main character, is a typically autobiographical story. Kacherin has the feeling that he is isolated and can't communicate with his parents. Questioning the purpose of life and oppressed by a sense of sin, he hopes that the Easter festival may give him an answer. His family do not seem to be interested in him, his only friend lets him down, and he is worried because he drinks secretly. When everyone goes to church without him he feels 'like Cain'; 'The whole world of people and things was talking in the same happy harmonious language. Only Kacherin didn't understand this language and was tor-

mented by a terrible sense of loneliness'. At the
end of the story Kacherin's mood does change,
when he sees a pretty girl, and he eventually
regains a sense of unity with the world. Another
lucky hero who also experiences happiness after
years of dissatisfaction is a student, Chistyakov,
in *The Foreigner* (1902). His one aim in life is
to save enough money to leave Russia, which
he hates, and he lives apart from the other
students. However, he is so impressed by the
intense longing of a Serbian student for his
homeland, that he gives the Serb his savings,
and then after this act of self-sacrifice is rewarded by a new love for Russia. It has been
suggested that *The Foreigner* was written by
Andreyev as a response to an appeal by Gorky.
'Today's young people want to read something
inspiring, heroic and even with some roman-
ticism'. In the story the Serb, Raiko Vukich, is
a romantic character, singing of his homeland
and suffering people, more like one of Gorky's
own characters.

It is much more common in Andreyev's
stories for the hero not to be able to achieve
any sort of escape from his isolation and un-
happiness, and this is one reason why critics
soon began to call Andreyev a pessimist, although there is no evidence that he held the
view that suffering was inevitable – a way out
is usually implied. Lack of communication

between parents and children is the theme of two stories written in December 1900. A number of preliminary drafts of the first of these, *Silence*, have been preserved, and are an interesting illustration of the development of Andreyev's technique. At first the story had a fairly complicated plot about the reasons why Vera, a priest's daughter, commits suicide. Andreyev gradually cuts out details and superfluous characters, so that the narrative concentrates on expressing the idea of silence. Vera's suicide is described in the finished story in one sentence. All the images reinforce the description of the silence which surrounds her father, a severe, cold man. 'Silence stifled him; it rolled past his head in icy waves and ruffled his hair; it beat against his breast which groaned under the blows'. Thus silence seems to be a kind of punishment for this cold intellectual priest, whose pride prevented him from communicating with his daughter. The second story, *Into The Dark Distance*, is about a family whose son, Nikolai, presumably rebelling against the restricted life of the older generation, leaves home for some mysterious other existence. His unexplained return home seven years later brings no joy to the family and they are oppressed by his presence. Andreyev compares Nikolai to an eagle—a symbol of unfettered freedom. (Gorky had used this image in his story *Old Izergil*.) He has broken away from his bourgeois family and now has nothing in common with them. It is not clear what he finds in 'the dark menacing distance' to which he returns at the end of the story, but Gorky and other critics saw him as a romantic hero, a revolutionary. Andreyev does not make this explicit and was probably more interested in describing the psychological effect on the family of being confronted with their son, who represents undiluted freedom—a threat to their secure conventional world.

Another subject which Andreyev investigated in stories at this time was death, probably influenced by his reading of Schopenhauer and Tolstoy. In the story *The Grand Slam* death punishes people who want to exclude the world and real life from their private 'fortress' (as the hero of *At the Window* called it.) *The Grand Slam* describes four people who spend their lives playing *vint* (a game very similar to bridge). The subject matter may have been suggested to Andreyev by Chekhov's well-known story of 1898, *A Man in a Case*. This describes a schoolmaster whose whole life is lived strictly according to rules, which form a case around him, just as he keeps his watch in a case, and his umbrella in a case. Chekhov's story ends with the words, 'Isn't the fact that we live in cities, write unnecessary papers and play *vint*, isn't this a case?' Andreyev's characters pass their days in a routine of card playing, never varying partners or positions at the table. Only one of them has any interest in the outside world, but when he tries to talk about the famous Dreyfus case, or his son who has been arrested for political activity, the others are not interested. The cards have come to dominate the four completely, and even Nikolai Dmitriyevich easily forgets about the outside world, in his eagerness to make a grand slam. On a fatal day, the only one distinguished in the story from the automatic passing of the seasons—the 26th November—he is dealt an unusually good hand and bids a grand slam in no trumps, but immediately dies from a heart attack, ironically never knowing that all the tricks were his. Life has avenged itself on the players, who ignored it, but they have not understood the danger. 'Where shall we find a fourth now?' is their response.

At the beginning of 1901 Andreyev spent some time in a Moscow clinic, recovering from nervous exhaustion and the effects of a prolonged drinking bout. His experiences there gave him material for one of his best early stories, *Once There Lived*, which he sketched out while still in hospital. This study of the death of two men was highly praised by most critics who saw it as a work in the realist tra-

dition of Russian literature, inspired by Tolstoy's *The Death of Ivan Il'ich*. Ward Eight,
where two middle aged men are dying, is spot-
lessly clean (unlike Chekhov's squalid Ward
No. 6 in the story of that name) and its whiteness is somehow sinister. 'The walls looked on
with the same cold indifference, and there was
a strange melancholy mockery in their irre-
proachable whiteness'. Once admitted to the
clinic, the men are in a kind of condemned cell.
The inscriptions over their beds are like those
on tombstones, and doctors use their bodies as
examples to illustrate lectures to medical students, reading out their case histories like
obituaries. One of the men, a merchant, is
gloomy and introverted but he finds it easier
to accept the fact that he will soon die than the
sociable, friendly deacon. Andreyev in this story
builds up a sense of routine, of ordered life in
the ward, a calm, antiseptic background against
which life gradually and inevitably flows out
of the two men. A third patient, a student,
recovers thanks to the visits of his pretty girl
friend, and a contemporary critic remarked
that this was the first example of a happy love
story in Andreyev's writing. A comment like
this shows that critics were still expecting
Andreyev to write stories with plots conform-
ing to some conventional scheme.

One of the most ambitious stories Andreyev

wrote in 1900 in both subject matter and length was *The Story of Sergei Petrovich*. It is the only story which has direct references to a philosopher—Nietzsche. Sergei Petrovich is a student who feels lonely at university and imagines that he is intellectually inferior to his fellows. He is also afraid that he may lose his individuality, and that he is just a statistic in society. The only moments in his life when Sergei was happy, had been spent away from the university doing manual work. However, he feels obliged to return to his studies to live up to his education and his parents' expectations. One day he reads *Thus Spake Zarathustra* and is very excited by the idea of the superman. Once Sergei shuts himself up in his room with his copy of Nietzsche, isolating himself from the outside world, tragedy is inevitable. He feels he must somehow assert his individuality, and reads Zarathustra's words: 'For many a man life is a failure; a poison worm eats at his heart. So let him see to it that his death is all the more a success'. This suggests to Sergei that suicide is the only thing in which he can be a superman. In this way Andreyev shows how excessive egoism is a destructive force, as in many of his stories. If the characters can overcome their self-preoccupation they can experience happiness and a sense of harmony with the world. *The Story of Sergei Petrovich* can be criticised for being too lengthy—Andreyev never imitated Chekhov's concise sentences—but on the other hand Andreyev's personal memories of contemplating suicide give the story some passion.

Three shorter stories are characteristic of Andreyev's attempts to break away from plots and concentrate on the expression of mood. *Deception* (1900) and *Laughter* (1901) both take the same situation, the love of a young man for a girl who doesn't take his passion seriously. These stories may have been prompted by Andreyev's own experiences, but they are in no sense realistic descriptions of events. Falseness is the theme in *Deception*, expressed by a student's inability to tell whether the girl he loves is lying when she says loves him. The student kills the girl, and then realises that he has 'immortalised the lie'. While at St. Petersburg University Andreyev had made several entries in his diary worrying over the problem of ever being able to know oneself properly, let alone other people, and for many years he puzzled over the ambiguity of truth. In *Laughter*, a student thwarted in love arrives at a party given by his girl, wearing a ridiculous mask. This provokes her to helpless laughter, and is a symbol of the gulf between people and their basic lack of communication. The student thinks, 'How far away was the world from me.

How lonely I was under this mask'. Masks are used by Andreyev as representations of the deceitful nature of people many times in later stories and plays.

The Wall (1901) is Andreyev's first attempt at writing a story which has no realistic basis. The setting is purely fantastic and allegorical. Lepers and diseased, degraded human beings stand in perpetual darkness before a massive wall, and try to climb it or knock it down. Andreyev later explained the symbolism of the wall in a letter to a woman reader: 'The Wall is everything that stands in the way of a new, perfect and happy life both in Russia and the West. It is social and political oppression, the imperfection of human nature, with its diseases, animal instincts, evil, greed etc; it is questions about the purpose and meaning of life, about God, life and death, the "accursed questions". The people before the wall are mankind fighting for truth, happiness and freedom'. Here we have a very explicit statement of the ideals Andreyev is putting forward in his stories. Man would like to find the way to the new life, but is hindered by external factors—lack of political freedom, and almost more than this by his own inadequacies, and his failure to find any answer to the 'accursed questions'. The images of *The Wall* are admittedly mainly horrible, suggesting that the animal side of human nature will never let mankind push over the wall, but there is a faint ray of hope in the narrator's suggestion that if the corpses of the sufferers are piled up against the wall, then the last man alive will see over it. The manner of *The Wall* may well have been suggested by Gorky's prose poem, *The Song of the Stormy Petrel*, published six months earlier. This was a much more specific political allegory, full of romantic optimism, and it had a tremendous success amongst young people. Stylistically, the two are not unalike, although Andreyev does not use Gorky's rhythmic prose, and writes at much greater length. Gorky uses images of turbulent clouds, winds and waves to represent the storm which is building up, and Andreyev too brings in the elements. He describes the night, the wind, and a sea of sorrow breaking against the wall. He repeats words and phrases as Gorky does, and later this was to become one of the most characteristic devices of his prose.

At some point in 1900 Andreyev decided that he would like some of his best stories re-published in a collection which would help him to become better known and bring in more money. He found it difficult to find a publisher at first, as his reputation had not yet gone much beyond readers of *The Courier* and *Everybody's Journal*. Eventually one editor paid him an advance, but the months passed and his book didn't appear. Meanwhile Gorky had joined the board of a publishing house in St. Petersburg, *Znaniye* (Knowledge) which was run as a co-operative venture. *Znaniye* agreed to publish Andreyev's stories, and in September 1901 the volume came out, dedicated to Gorky. It was an immediate success, and Andreyev wrote later to a friend, 'In some four months I had climbed to the peak of literary fame. The number of favourable reviews took up much more space than the book itself'. The first printing sold 4,000 copies, and the second of 8,000 copies sold out in two weeks. Eventually 47,000 copies were printed, a record figure for the time, and Andreyev earned 6,000 roubles in the first year alone. In the second edition, An-dreyev added six more stories to the original ten, including *The Wall*, and *The Abyss*, written in 1902, which was to provoke a good deal of controversy. The venerable literary critic N. K. Mikhailovsky congratulated Andreyev on the volume, and set an official seal of approval on his work. Andreyev could now consider himself an established writer.

Chapter III

The Abyss

Andreyev was thirty when his first collection of stories was published, and he now was entering the most successful and happy period of his life. The constant worry about money which had oppressed him since the age of seventeen had disappeared, and he was able to move into a better flat, spend fairly lavishly on hospitality and buy new clothes. Andreyev enjoyed his sudden fame, and was flattered by the stream of distinguished visitors who now came to see him. He was confident enough to invite members of the Wednesday circle to meet at his flat. Fame had unpleasant consequences as well, and Andreyev began to experience the kind of adverse publicity in the newspapers which was to distress him for the rest of his life. Improved communications of the twentieth century had made it easier for a writer to become famous almost overnight, but there was also the new risk that malicious journalism could destroy reputations just as quickly. A report in a provincial newspaper that Andreyev and his fiancée had been seen swimming in the nude was the first example of many subsequent false allegations about the writer. In February 1902 Andreyev married Alexandra Veligorskaya, an attractive, rather shy girl, whose charm and elegance delighted everyone who met her. The marriage was very happy, and Andreyev from now on refused to be separated from Alexandra. He only accepted invitations which included her, and Alexandra for her part devoted herself entirely to caring for her husband, acting as secretary and critic as well as being a devoted wife. She would often stay up all night, while Andreyev wrote, and then listen to his stories. If she suggested alterations, Andreyev would rewrite whole pages. Alexandra made sure that trivial domestic cares did not bother her husband, and was able to persuade him to cut down his drinking and reassure him when he was depressed. Alexandra must have been very tactful, avoiding friction with Andreyev's mother, who was still determined to perform many services for her adored son.

The success of his collection of stories seems to have given Andreyev a new confidence to write about more controversial subjects and also to commit himself more to expressing his own ideas. Two stories written early in 1902 were to increase Andreyev's fame and also bring him some notoriety. He chose to write on sex and violence in a way which was outspoken for the time, and this provoked a violent reaction from some sections of the public. *In the Fog* (published in December 1902) was described as a 'harmful, pornographic work' by the editor of the very conservative paper *New Time*, and later the story had the distinction of being attacked by Countess Tolstoy (the writer's wife) in the same paper. (Anton Chekhov commented at the time that her letter could well be a forgery as the views it expressed were so reactionary.) This opposition, as usually happens, only ensured that more copies of the story were sold, and many younger writers rushed to defend Andreyev. One paper even arranged a questionnaire among its readers, asking for comments on Countess Tolstoy's objections. Most of the replies said that Andreyev has raised important questions, and that it was dangerous hypocrisy to ignore the existence of such problems.

The heroes of both stories are young men, one aged 18, the other 21, brought up in middle class families, who find themselves in situations where the rules they have been taught fail to curb their basic sexual instincts. *The Abyss* opens with a picture of idealistic young love inspired by literature and high-minded sentiment. Nemovetsky, who is 21, is walking one evening in the country with Zinochka (whose name reminds us of Andreyev's unhappy love for Zinaida ten years previously.) The couple are so wrapped up in each other that gradually

45

they lose their way, and Andreyev changes the lyrical mood of the story to one of horror and fear. The beginning of the story is based on Andreyev's memories of the Orel countryside and his own schoolboy love, but the end turns to fantasy, or perhaps a wish to illustrate Schopenhauer's idea of the sexual impulse as a 'demon that strives to pervert, confuse and overthrow everything'. After sunset the landscape changes from a lyrical echo of the couple's love to a menacing and threatening force. The clouds take on monstrous shapes, hideous prostitutes sit by the roadside, and the pleasant dream fades before the darkness and dirt of the real world. Three drunks attack the couple, beat up Nemovetsky and leave him unconscious, and then rape Zinochka. When Nemovetsky comes round he discovers the girl lying semi-conscious stripped of her clothes. Although he struggles to treat her as before, when a delicate squeeze of the hand seemed daring, he cannot control his own passion, and rapes Zinochka himself. 'In the force and anguish of the kiss he lost the last sparks of reason. For a single instant flaming horror lighted up his mind, opening before him a black abyss, and the black abyss swallowed him'. Andreyev implies that Nemovetsky's upbringing had been too unrealistic, and the boy had not learned to recognise the dark force of his sexuality. Public debate about

The Abyss was so widespread that a caricature of Andreyev balancing over a chasm was produced as a picture postcard.

In the Fog puts its young hero, Pavel, in an even more unpleasant situation. The fog of the title, which blankets the city, reflects the confusion and shame which Pavel feels, and the lack of communication with his family. Pavel has not been able to make a satisfactory relationship with a girl of his own age and social class. He is obsessed by a girl called Katya, who knows nothing of his love and flirts with other boys, greatly distressing Pavel. Yet Pavel has to endure more than loneliness and unrequited love, for he has been visiting prostitutes in secret, a common practice amongst his school friends, and has contracted a venereal disease. He can tell no one about this, and is tormented by shame. Meanwhile Pavel's father has been shocked by the discovery of an obscene drawing, obviously made by his son. The father is described as a well-meaning, conventional man, an insurance inspector for the Phoenix company. He thinks he is enlightened, but shows a disastrous incompetence when he tries to talk to Pavel about sex. His pompous generalisations get nowhere near an understanding of Pavel's agonised state of mind, and the gulf between father and son is fixed for ever. Driven to desperation by the feeling that he is besmirched and can never fit into family life again, Pavel walks out into the city streets, murky in the yellow fog. He picks up a prostitute, goes to her room and gets very drunk, and his basic instincts take over. 'He saw only the body, a woman's body, frightening and incomprehensible in its power. He had dreamed about such a body, found it repulsive enough to want to trample it with his feet, and yet as desirable as water in a puddle for a man dying of thirst.' Pavel kills the woman, and then commits suicide.

Sex in these stories is as destructive a force as Tolstoy suggested in *The Kreutzer Sonata*, but Andreyev doesn't draw Tolstoy's moral that universal chastity is the only solution. Andreyev is more concerned with expressing the intensity of his characters' experience, and by placing them in extreme situations, tests them. If they prove themselves to be weak, it is partly the fault of society for not equipping them to deal with these situations, and partly a failure to understand the force of the unconscious part of their minds. *The Abyss* was attacked in the press for its 'immorality', and Gorky noticed how upset Andreyev was by the public scandal over the story. Andreyev answered some of the attacks in an article printed in *The Courier* in January 1902. He admitted that there might be artistic faults in the story, 'artificiality, mannerism, an obvious wish to intensify the sense of horror, a psychologically weak ending', but he refused to admit that it was a slander on human nature. Modern man, in Andreyev's view, had acquired only the outer forms of culture, but at heart had remained an animal in a large part of his impulses and instincts. His conclusion is that a society which still encouraged prostitution was in no position to criticise Nemovetsky.

Again Andreyev was accused of being a pessimist, and his stories of 1902 and 1903 do on the whole have gloomy conclusions. His much happier and more stable personal life did not affect the mood of his writing, but outside his fiction, Andreyev several times affirmed his faith in life. In an article called *The Wild Duck*, inspired by a current production of Ibsen's play in Moscow (1902), Andreyev wrote: 'I never believe so much in life, as when I am reading the "father of pessimism" Schopenhauer. A man thought in that way and lived. That means that life is powerful and victorious'. Schopenhauer's ideas continued to attract Andreyev throughout his life. He wrote to Gorky in August 1904, 'Have you read *The World as Will and Idea*? I'm under the spell of this splendid book. It's so clever, beautiful and elegant. It's possible that I haven't understood Schopenhauer quite correctly, and have interpreted him as I want myself'. It is true that Andreyev often alters Schopenhauer's ideas to suit his own thinking, but as we have seen in the two stories just discussed, the idea of strong drives in a person, which he may not fully understand, can be traced to Schopenhauer's concept of *will*, or as his disciple Eduard von Hartmann had already called it by 1869, *the unconscious* (some years before Freud used the term). Writing on aesthetics Schopenhauer said, 'a novel will be the higher and nobler the more inner and less outer life it depicts', and this statement could certainly be taken as one of Andreyev's principles of literary composition.

A young writer, Boris Zaitsev, was one of the visitors to Andreyev's flat in the early 1900s who noticed how the writer's living standards were improving. Like many other people he was very impressed by Andreyev's appearance and personality, 'I was really hypnotised by him. I liked everything about the man and his writings'. Zaitsev described the pattern of Andreyev's life at that time. He used to get up late and drink glass after glass of tea throughout the day. Any visitors who arrived were drawn into long conversations about God, death, literature, revolution and war. (Andreyev was a tireless conversationalist—Gorky remembered talking to him once for twenty hours.) Andreyev smoked all the time, and used to walk up and

50

down while he talked, in a rather nervous way. He joked very easily in conversation, but as Zaitsev noticed, this humour never found its way into his fiction. The family would have a meal at 3 p.m., and then Andreyev would sleep until about 8 p.m., drink some strong tea and write for hours, often until dawn. Nothing could distract him if he was in the middle of a story, and he seemed to write with a kind of feverish intoxication. Andreyev always gave the impression of being excited and animated to his friends, and rarely seemed tired.

Andreyev's friendship with Gorky continued to deepen, and they frequently visited each other during this period. 1902 was the year that Gorky was elected an honorary academician of the Imperial Academy of Sciences, as a mark of his literary distinction, but because of Gorky's record of political protest Nicholas II objected to the election, and it was annulled by the government. Chekhov and Korolenko then resigned from the Academy in protest, and the incident caused a great stir. As a close friend of the famous Maxim Gorky, Andreyev must have felt that he was very much at the centre of literary politics. Many people imagined that he would sooner or later follow Gorky's example, and involve himself in political activity. Andreyev, however, never committed himself, although at that time he was no supporter of the autocracy, and was sympathetic to plans for revolution. It was not so much the risk of joining a party and possible imprisonment which deterred Andreyev—he was never lacking in personal courage—but rather his own temperament. From his schooldays on, Andreyev never joined groups of any kind, and was always acutely aware of himself as an isolated individual. The Wednesday circle was an exception, and Andreyev remained loyal to it probably because its approval gave him confidence in his early days as a writer. No outsiders were allowed into the circle, and the rule was that all the members had to be frank and not be offended by criticism. After a year or two as a member, Andreyev in fact became the most regular contributor of new stories. One contemporary writer, Veresayev, who used to attend some of the meetings thought that Andreyev had a rather lazy temperament, and that it was this that allowed him to remain associated with the realist writers for some time after he had ceased to agree with their approach to literature. Veresayev first met Andreyev in 1903 and noted his 'piercing eyes', beard and thick mane of hair, and remembers how Andreyev enjoyed telling one story against him-self—his dark good looks and unconventional dress had led to him being mistaken for another Andreyev, the conductor of a band of gypsy singers. Veresayev also thought that Andreyev was rather ignorant about politics and didn't try to widen his horizons once he became famous. There may have been some truth in this and Gorky more than once complained that Andreyev did not read enough, but the latter never had Gorky's thirst for self education.

An important story written in 1902 by Andreyev was *Thought*, summarising some of the ideas he had been expressing in earlier stories about man's intellect. Andreyev shared in the general distrust of rationalism at the end of the nineteenth century, and the belief that certain things could only be understood intuitively. A typical expression of this was the philosophy of Henri Bergson, which was extremely popular during the first years of the century. 'The intellect is characterised by a natural inability to understand life', said Bergson, and Andreyev had acquired a similar distrust of the intellect through his reading of Schopenhauer, and from what he had absorbed of symbolist theories. The heroes of Andreyev's stories are nearly all limited by trust in their own powers of reasoning, and to achieve any peace of mind they must somehow transcend their egoism. In *Thought* the main character, Doctor Kerzhentsev, has no doubts about the superiority of his intellect, and exults in the power of his thought. 'My thoughts and I literally played with life

and death and soared high above them'. The
story is in the form of notes made by the doctor
as he plans and carries out a murder. Kerzhentsev has decided to avenge his slighted feelings,
because a woman who refused to marry him is
now happily married to another. Comparing
himself to Raskolnikov in Dostoyevsky's *Crime
and Punishment*, Kerzhentsev plans and carries
out what is to be a perfect murder of the lady's
present husband. Kerzhentsev's plan is to pre-
tend to be mad, and to be acquitted of the
murder on the grounds of insanity. However,
once he has actually committed the crime he
suffers a breakdown, and finds that his thoughts
are no longer under his control. Kerzhentsev
now doubts his own sanity, and sees his mistake
in relying on his intellect. 'I was betrayed...
My castle became my prison. Enemies attacked
me in my castle. Where is there any escape?
My ruin lies in the impregnability of my castle
and the thickness of its walls. Who is strong
enough to save me? No one. For there is no one
stronger than I, and I am the only enemy of
my "I"'. The image of a castle in this story to
represent Kerzhentsev's mind is typical of Andreyev's choice of walls, fortresses and prisons
as an expression of the various restrictions
people build round themselves. Kerzhentsev
staked everything on his intellect, but this
proved a trap from which he could not escape.

The story puzzled some of those who read it for the first time—Mikhailovsky rejected it for publication in his journal *Russian Will*, and wrote to Andreyev saying that he didn't understand the ideas behind *Thought*. Chekhov read it and described the story as pretentious and obscure, although he admitted that the writing was competent, and continued, 'There's no simplicity in Andreyev, and his talent reminds me of the singing of a clockwork nightingale'. Gorky read the proofs of *Thought* and at that time was enthusiastic about the story, especially approving the concluding word 'Nothing!' However, later on Gorky changed his mind, calling it entirely pessimistic, perhaps rather annoyed by Andreyev's admission that Savelov, the murdered husband, was partly a portrait of Gorky himself. Andreyev told Gorky, 'There is one sentence—"Alexei wasn't talented". Perhaps I shouldn't have written it, but you irritate me so much with your stubbornness sometimes that you seem stupid'. Despite criticism, Andreyev more than once returned to the ideas he was trying to express in *Thought*, and rewrote the story as a play in 1914. Andreyev's writing is always on a very serious level. He wanted to put forward important ideas about human nature and society, and the enthusiasms of his personal life, his love of wife and family, enjoyment of nature and painting, and his sense of humour, are hardly ever reflected in his stories.

In 1903 Andreyev published fewer stories, partly because he was composing a much longer work, *The Life of Vasili Fiveisky*, completed in November of that year and published in the first *Znaniye* almanac. At this time much new writing was published in annual almanacs or miscellanies, collections of prose and poetry selected by editors of the various publishing houses. *Znaniye* included Andreyev's story, and among other things, a brief prose-poem by Gorky called *Man*, the mood of which is in sharp contrast to Andreyev's story. *Man* is highly optimistic in tone, full of Gorky's belief in the power of human beings to create a new society for themselves. It is interesting to note that Gorky stressed the word *Thought* (always written with a capital letter in his poem) as one of the most valuable attributes of man, helping him to win the battle for freedom. *Man* could have been written as a refutation of Andreyev's story *Thought*, as here Gorky praises the rationality of human beings, with no misgivings about any subconscious forces. *Man* is equally far from the mood of *Vasili Fiveisky*, the tragic story of a village priest who loses his reason. Stories about the clergy were not uncommon at that date—there was one called *In the Parish* in the same *Znaniye* almanac—but the writers were usually attacking abuses in the church, and describing priests who either helped the peasants or exploited them. Andreyev's story was very different in its emphasis, for it is not concerned with describing the way of life of a typical village priest, a subject about which Andreyev had no specialised knowledge. As usual Andreyev concentrates on ideas and this very dramatic story is concerned with a crisis in one man's mind.

The Life of Vasili Fiveisky describes a few years in the career of Father Vasili, during which fate, described as 'menacing, mysterious' deals him blow after blow, as if trying to undermine his stubborn faith in God. Father Vasili marries, has two children, and all seems well for a time. When his young son is drowned accidentally, his wife is so distressed by the tragedy that she starts drinking heavily, and the priest discovers that his daughter is just the same sort of cold, unloving person that he himself is. Andreyev's prose is heavily charged with exaggerated images to reinforce the sense of desperation and chaos that surround Father Vasili. The priest and his wife live in an atmosphere of menace. 'Cut off by the walls and the night from people and life, they seemed to be spinning in a nightmarish whirlwind. Wild cries and curses spun round with them. Madness itself stood at the door, and the air was hot

with its breath'. Father Vasili's house is a
projection of his self, like Kerzhentsev's castle,
and Andreyev describes the elements—winds
and snow storms battering at it, as if trying to
break down his façade of rationality. A second
son born to Father Vasili as a result of his
alcoholic wife's 'mad passion' is mentally defec-
tive, and as he grows older reveals an evil temperament. The idiot son may be taken as a
symbol of the animal side of Father Vasili's
nature, or of his corrupting faith in his intellect.
Faith in God for Vasili is intellectual—an
assertion of belief despite misfortunes. He is
feverishly searching for the truth, another
preoccupation of Andreyev's heroes, and spends
hours in the confessional, cross questioning his
parishioners. More tragedies follow; Father
Vasili's wife is burnt to death, all his possessions
are lost, his daughter is sent away, and the
priest builds himself a squalid house where he
lives alone with the imbecile. Father Vasili now
comes to regard himself as chosen by God,
because of the exceptional suffering he has
endured. He reasons that he is to be God's
instrument in the performance of a miracle or
an heroic deed. The story ends very dramatic-
ally, and Andreyev uses his most hyperbolic
style to describe the church filled with believers,
and a coffin with a decomposing body. A violent
thunderstorm is taking place and images of

darkness dominate. Father Vasili decides that the time for the miracle has arrived, and he tries to resurrect the corpse by commanding it to rise. He fails, and then goes mad, his faith in God lost, with a vision of the church collapsing around him like the walls of his mind. (Here Andreyev may have been inspired by the closing scenes of Poe's *The Fall of the House of Usher*.) He rushes out into the fields, and, as if escaping from dark forces, runs until he dies.

Andreyev considered *Vasili Fiveisky* an important story and worked on it for several months trying to achieve the right tone. He changed the title several times, and unsuccessfully tried to alter the last four pages, while it was already in the press, in order to make Father Vasili seem more rebellious. Generally it was favourably reviewed, although Andreyev was accused by some critics of making Vasili suffer too much, and the church disapproved of atheistic ideas in the story. Andreyev explained to one critic his ideas about the problems he tackled in the story. 'Take a man who believes deeply and sees God as the God of Love and Justice. If you can prove to this fervent believer that the next world is the same as this, and that there will be no solutions, then he will cease to believe. Belief that it is possible to find justice and a purpose in life is a fallacy'. Gorky approved of the story as an attack on the

Orthodox church, and wrote to the editor of the almanac, 'Andreyev hasn't written so well as this before'. Although *Vasili Fiveisky* lacks polish and is too drawn out, it was written with passion, and this was transmitted to contemporary readers. When the story was finished Andreyev read it aloud to Shalyapin, the famous singer, a member of the Wednesday circle, and the latter wept. Alexander Blok, one of the best known symbolist poets, was also deeply moved by the story and spoke of its meaning for him: 'I knew long ago, before the first revolution, that the catastrophe was near, and that horror was at the gates, and *The Life of Vasili Fiveisky* accorded with my sense of foreboding'.

These remarks by Blok indicate that Andreyev's art reflected the mood of many people in Russia, and also how he seemed to be moving nearer to the symbolists at this time in his attempts to describe hidden forces in the mind of man, and to go behind the world of appearances. Yet Andreyev was always conscious that he didn't belong to a particular literary school. In 1912 he wrote to Gorky asking, 'Who am I? For the well-born decadents I am a despised realist, while for the hereditary realists, a suspect symbolist'. The reference to well-born writers reminds us that Andreyev was conscious that he had not come from the fairly wealthy background which was still typical of many writers—Gorky being a notable exception—and sometimes felt at a disadvantage in their company. However, in the tense atmosphere of 1903 the differences mattered less. Blok wrote that all writers were in some ways hysterical during the first decade of the twentieth century, and that Andreyev's stories all burned with this madness. Andreyev's writing for the next few years was in tune with historical events.

Chapter IV

War and Revolution

At the beginning of 1904 the outbreak of war with Japan added a new impetus to demands for reform in Russia. The government ministers who had urged Nicholas II to declare war, some hoping to gain ports and spheres of interest in the Far East, and others wanting to divert public attention from a revolutionary situation at home, had given little forethought to the problems involved. They expected an easy victory, but the war, conducted thousands of miles from St. Petersburg, with only a single track railway line to ensure supplies, in fact turned out to be a series of disastrous defeats, and many people came to feel that the autocracy rather than Japan was the real enemy. Andreyev shared in the general revulsion for the war, and by November 1904 had completed a story based on it, which proved to be immensely popular.

During the summer of 1904 Andreyev took his family to the Crimean resort of Yalta, but even there could not have avoided reading the daily newspaper reports of bloody battles and retreats in Manchuria. The Russian army was continually outmanoeuvred by a smaller, more efficient Japanese force, who, in contrast to their opponents, were well prepared for the war. One day Andreyev happened to witness an injured workman carried past his house on a stretcher (after an explosion nearby). The sight of the mutilated body brought home the reality of war to Andreyev, and soon he had planned his story *The Red Laugh*. He worked feverishly on it, and completed the first draft in nine days. (The story is 52 pages long in the close type of the 1913 edition). He was so absorbed in the story that he literally exhausted himself mentally and physically, and afterwards found that he could not write again for several months, so vividly had he seemed to live through the scenes he described. He recuperated by intense physical activity —cycling, swimming and boating— and re-read the adventure stories he had enjoyed as a boy, by Jules Verne and Alexandre Dumas.

Andreyev of course had no first hand experience of the war, but this did not deter him from describing events at the front line. Strict accuracy in reporting battles was less important to Andreyev than evoking the sense of chaos and the apparent triumph of the animal instincts of man in war. Some critics attacked him for the lack of realism in the story and exaggeration of the horrors of war. Veresayev, who had graduated from a medical faculty and had been at the front as a doctor, recalled that copies of *The Red Laugh* arrived during the battle of Mukden, when the army was suffering appalling losses, but the men who read it merely laughed at its imaginary horrors. Veresayev, who wrote stories and polemical articles attacking the government for embarking on such a senseless war, implied that Andreyev was a defeatist. Gorky read the story, and predictably suggested alterations which would make it more realistic, but Andreyev did not take his advice. *The Red Laugh* is an experimental work in which Andreyev was seeking a form which would express his ideas more forcefully. The story is subtitled 'Fragments from a discovered manuscript', and every fragment (except one) begins half way through a sentence. The first words 'madness and horror' are to be repeated many times in the story and are the key to Andreyev's interpretation of war. He intended the story to be a psychological picture of war, and an analysis of its destructive effect on the human psyche. Thus the fragments are full of nightmarish pictures of the horror of war, which causes people either to go mad or to lose all civilised values. The reader has no idea where this war is taking place, nor whose armies are involved, and this emphasises Andreyev's wish to give the story universal significance, rather than make it a specific protest against a particular war. At the end of the second fragment the *red laugh* is introduced as a symbol of the bestiality in men which allows them to wage war, and this image is repeated many times in the story.

The picture of life at the front is a very terrible one. There is no relief from the harsh landscape and the burning heat. (Andreyev had found the climate of the Crimea unbearably hot, and returned to Moscow early, in the middle of August 1904.) To the usual discomforts of war—dirt, hunger, fatigue, vermin and administrative mistakes—Andreyev adds his own metaphysical horror. The narrator says: 'I recognised the red laugh. I had sought and found this red laugh. Now I understood what was in all those mutilated, torn, alien bodies. It was the red laugh. It is in the sky and the sun, and soon it will pour out over the whole earth'. In fragment seven, which Gorky thought should be excluded because it could be used as a demonstration of Japanese atrocities, it is implied that a Red Cross train of patients is blown up. In the following fragment, the narrator, who has lost both legs, is back home again, but the horror and madness has returned with him to the city. Soon the narrator cracks up and goes mad, writing feverishly for two months with a dry pen, until his death. His brother takes over the narrative, giving a picture of the city

66

as it is affected by the war, full of crazed soldiers returning from the front, and shocking daily newspaper reports. The brother is similarly affected by the horror of the situation. 'I'm beginning to think that the moment of world catastrophe is approaching'. The conclusion of the story is a terrible vision of corpses being spewed out of the earth in ever increasing numbers, covering the ground and stifling the narrator and his family—the triumph of the red laugh. These details seem artificial and grotesque, and Gorky objected to the ending, writing to Andreyev: 'It doesn't come off. Ezekiel describes this more beautifully and more terribly. You must stop somewhere earlier…. The facts are more terrible and more significant than your attitude toward them in this case'. Andreyev did not take Gorky's advice. He had experienced the mood of the story so intensely while writing it that he could not look at it objectively.

The experimental form of *The Red Laugh* does not entirely succeed in conveying Andreyev's hatred of war, perhaps partly because of the vague characterisation of the narrator. The reader only discovers half-way through the story that the apparently first-hand experiences of the officer at the front have in fact been composed by his brother. Vasili Fiveisky's long struggle seems by contrast more effective because we are more personally involved with him. In addition, the writer's best stories are never free from a certain dependence on dramatic events, and in *The Red Laugh* where the author strives to express a more general mood of horror emotional impact is lessened. Despite defects which may deter a modern reader, the story was an immediate success when published, and 60,000 copies were sold of the *Znaniye* almanac in which it was published. For Andreyev's contemporaries it expressed something of the extreme dissatisfaction caused by the war, and the pent up feelings of years of cruel repression. *The Red Laugh* was generally seen as an argument for pacifism, following in Tolstoy's footsteps. Tolstoy had been arguing against war for two decades, and by now had a large number of supporters. Andreyev sent Tolstoy a copy of the story, and admitted that he found it difficult to express his repugnance of war. Perhaps that is why the story was—as Andreyev admitted—too artificial in structure and details. Tolstoy agreed about its artificiality, and wrote that he found it vague, but thought it could be useful in its present form in the cause of peace.

The continuing disasters of the war led directly to the revolutionary events of 1905, when it seemed for a time that Russia might at last gain a constitution. Andreyev was as excited as most other intellectuals and felt that a new Russia was being created. One evening in February of that year he willingly lent his flat for a meeting of important members of the marxist Social Democratic party, which was still illegal. The police were informed in advance and Andreyev's flat was raided. Together with the nine marxists, and the writer Skitalets who had called by chance, Andreyev was arrested and taken to prison. Naturally the arrest of a popular writer aroused a lot of protest in the country, and Andreyev received quite good treatment. The Taganka prison where he spent two weeks, was overflowing with distinguished political offenders and Andreyev enjoyed the company. He wrote in his diary that he slept soundly the first night in prison, and found the cell and food rather better than the living standards he had experienced as a student. The day of his arrest was his third wedding anniversary, and his diary entries referred affectionately to his wife and small son Vadim, regretting this disturbance in their lives. Newspapers were smuggled in to the prison and read aloud, and Andreyev recalled how much more interesting the articles seemed. He also told Gorky, 'My memories of prison are among my most pleasant ones. I felt really human'. Finally, after various representations Andreyev was let out on bail, and was never charged with any offence, but soon afterwards he found it necessary to make considerable changes in his life. He travelled to the Crimea again for the summer, but on his return to Moscow he found that he was in danger of being physically attacked by members of armed ultra-conservative groups known as the Black Hundreds, who rallied to the support of the autocracy. (Andreyev was on their black list as a writer with revolutionary sympathies.)

As it seemed dangerous to stay in Moscow the Andreyevs left for the comparative safety of Finland, then part of the Russian empire, but with some autonomy. Andreyev probably never imagined that it would be two years before he could return to Moscow. It was not a happy time, for Andreyev's youngest sister died that autumn at the age of 21 from a brain haemorrhage, and this deeply depressed him. Even Finland proved to be an insecure place for the family, and the Andreyevs left for Germany in November 1905 on their first visit to Western Europe. Andreyev was not impressed by what he found in Switzerland, Italy and Germany, and remained homesick for Russia. He wrote to a friend from Berlin in December, asking for full details about revolutionary events in Moscow, regretting that he could not be taking part. Andreyev complained at length about the Germans' excessive respect for order and their militarism. As Andreyev was no linguist, and never mastered a foreign language, Western Europe always seemed fairly alien to him. The following summer Andreyev went back to Finland, which was still seething with unrest. Here he was received as a representative of the Russian revolution, and invited to speak at public meetings. The writer Yevgeny Zamyatin went to hear him, and recalls how impressively Andreyev delivered his speech. Andreyev spoke solemnly, very much in the tone of his fiction. 'The seconds fall like drops. And with each second the head in the crown is nearer to the block. In a day, in three days, in a week, the last drop will fall, and the crown will clatter down the steps, followed by the head'. Further involvement with left wing groups in Finland eventually meant that Andreyev once again had to leave the country rapidly to escape arrest.

Despite all the personal and public disturbances of 1905, Andreyev started writing in the summer and produced a considerable amount of new work, although publication was delayed until the following year. The first draft of the story *Thus it Was* had in fact been finished in 1904. Gorky read it and suggested that the emphasis of the story should be changed, and this time Andreyev followed his advice, rewriting it in the summer of 1905. He read it aloud to the Wednesday circle before leaving Moscow. From its subject matter his audience took it to be a prediction of the failure of the revolution. However, Andreyev as usual was less concerned with specific political events than with generalisations about human nature. In *Thus it Was*, following Gorky's suggestion, Andreyev points to the slavishness in human beings, whose fondness for rules destroys their own freedom. The events of this story take place in an allegorical setting, without any identifiably Russian features, so that there are no obvious parallels with the current situation in Russia. A massive fortress which houses the twentieth king of a long line, stands on a rock, dominating and threatening the town. In this story Andreyev investigates the nature of power. Power has been passed from one king to another, and people accept it because it has always been there, and it seems to hypnotise them. A cynical refrain is made by the swishing of the pendulum of the huge tower clock, sounding like the words, 'Thus it was—this it will be'. Suddenly there is a revolution—'the mysterious revolt of millions is just as mysterious as the mysterious power of one man', comments the narrator. But the revolution is not very successful, because the centuries of respect for tyranny and the powerful slogan, 'Long live the twentieth' are deeply ingrained.

Traitors have to be executed in large numbers to save the revolution, and the king is brought to trial. In the dock he is revealed as a very ordinary, bourgeois small fat man with a bad cold. After his execution, however, ominous shouts of 'Long live the twenty first' are heard, and one of Andreyev's supernatural symbols broods over the town, 'something like a living cloud, huge, formless and blind'. The conclusion is that people do not really want freedom, and so the pendulum goes on swinging, because of man's inner slavishness. *Thus it Was* was published in 1906 in a new symbolist almanac, *Fakely (Torches)*, as the editors regarded Andreyev's allegorical stories as suitable material.

It would be wrong to infer from *Thus it Was* that Andreyev felt entirely pessimistic about all revolutionary activity. In two very brief stories we find a much more optimistic, romantic view. *The Marseillaise* (1903) describes a brief episode in which an apparently cowardly man dies bravely for the cause, and has the Marseillaise sung in his honour: 'We sang the great song of freedom with young strong voices, echoed by the ocean'. A similar optimism pervades *From a Story which will Not be Finished*, written in 1906, about a man who prepares to sacrifice himself manning the barricades, and feels inner inspiration and joy. These two stories describe men altruistically sacrificing themselves for a cause and thus experiencing a moment of happiness.

The most important story conceived and written in 1905 was *The Governor*. Andreyev was now entering his most fruitful and successful period as a writer, despite the fact that these four years were in fact the most unsettled of his life. He travelled extensively, had no permanent home and suffered personal tragedy. *The Governor*, based on various events which actually happened, was written in the summer of 1905 and published in the Social-Democrat journal *Pravda* in March 1906. The copy of *Pravda* was subsequently banned and confiscated because of the political content of the story. Andreyev based the story on the assassination of the Governor of Moscow, the Grand Duke Sergei Alexandrovich, in February 1905. He told his friend Veresayev that the motive for the Grand Duke's assassination was the public beating of demonstrators on the streets of Moscow two months previously. The Socialist Revolutionaries (the most extreme left wing group, responsible for many assassinations) literally sentenced the governor to death after the beatings, and this was widely known in advance. The shooting of demonstrators with which *The Governor* opens was no doubt taken from the events of Bloody Sunday in January 1905 when troops in St. Petersburg shot at peaceful marchers, killing and wounding hundreds. Andreyev at first called this story *The God of Vengeance*, and it is the aspect of revenge which in fact interests him, more than revolutionary activities. The story is a study of the governor's psychological condition in the short time he has left to live. Andreyev hoped to avoid censorship by putting the action in a provincial town, and changing the governor from an aristocratic figure to a fairly ordinary civil servant.

The dramatic episode which is responsible for the start of the governor's psychological disintegration is described in one paragraph. A demonstration seems to be getting out of control and the frightened governor gives orders to open fire. Later he views the corpses neatly laid out by a young policeman who takes great pride in his work. (This scene is very reminiscent of Tolstoy's satirical manner.) In fact the governor hardly needs to be sentenced by the revolutionaries, for the memory of the terrible slaughter haunts him and he can't escape. 'Thought was killing him. It summoned out of the darkness those who were to inflict the blow. It fashioned them like a creator'. The primitive force of revenge for the dead men takes shape of its own accord, and the governor bravely waits for death, not attempting to hide. Andreyev portrays him as a sympathetic character, not a rigid reactionary, but a sensitive man, who likes growing vegetables at his dacha, takes a long walk every day, and doesn't enjoy his power. Waiting to be assassinated he receives anonymous letters, and among them there is one which expresses what could be Andreyev's own view about revolutionary activities. A worker writes protesting against the use of political assassination in achieving revolutionary ideals. 'We must conquer by the head, and not by the hands'. The story ends with a typically Andreyevan image, 'the menacing form of the Law of Vengeance' hovers over the town, while people go on living their everyday lives.

Not all Andreyev's writing at this time was related to current events. One fairly slight work, *Christians*, which may well have been written to earn a little extra money—Andreyev never quite earned enough to keep up with his considerable expenditure—shows the writer in a more satirical mood, almost approaching humour. It is competently written, as were many of the other briefer stories which Andreyev continued to produce in addition to more ambitious works. *Christians* is very close to a typical Tolstoyan theme, and not unnaturally Tolstoy himself thought it was excellent. It is in a straightforward style, largely dialogue, very different from a story like *The Red Laugh*. This satire on the artificiality of the courts, and the ambiguity of conventional religion, recalls the writer's own legal experience. A witness in a court case refuses to take the oath, because she is a prostitute, and maintains that she cannot therefore be a Christian. Proceedings are held up while first lawyers and then a priest try to convince the woman that she *can* be a Christian but she wins by her obstinacy, and shows up the hypocrisy of the courts.

After fleeing from Finland in July 1906, Andreyev went back to Berlin. Alexandra was expecting their second child, and it was certainly not safe to return to Moscow, although he longed to be back there. Despite depressing news from Russia of the return of autocratic rule, Andreyev was absorbed by his writing during the autumn of 1906. Then quite suddenly tragedy struck the family. Alexandra gave birth to a boy in November 1906, and a few days later died from a post-natal infection. Andreyev was entirely crushed by this, and attacking the incompetence of the German doctors brought him no relief. It was feared that he might kill himself, but fortunately Gorky was able to help by suggesting that Andreyev should join him on Capri, where he was in exile. In a dark, gloomy villa which he rented, Andreyev gradually recovered, despite a return to heavy drinking, helped by the natural beauty of the island, and the sea which he particularly loved. Some months later he was telling his friends that he would have to re-marry. Alexandra, who understood his need for feminine company and support, even suggested this to him as she was dying, urging him to keep on writing.

Andreyev's preoccupation with death appears again in *Lazarus*, written in August 1906. *Lazarus* has a biblical setting, and a style very similar to Andreyev's earlier allegorical stories. Gorky wrote from Capri with enthusiasm, 'This is the best of all that has been written about death in all the world's literature, ...but philosophically I can't accept it'. The style of *Lazarus* is that of a simple folk tale, with a narrator relating and interpreting events. Lazarus has returned from the grave, and at first his friends do not pay sufficient attention to warning signs such as his changed character. Soon it becomes clear that Lazarus has returned as some sort of representative of death, hostile to life and human beings. He saps the will to live of anyone who meets his eyes, and infects them with his indifference. It is, as Andreyev puts it, as if 'the Ineffable Yonder' (nepostizhimoye tam) was looking at people through his gaze. Andreyev frequently repeats phrases in the story giving it a biblical, rhetorical tone. In the middle of the narrative there is an inserted prose poem, full of references to the 'horror of the Infinite', and to darkness and emptiness surrounding the world. Here Andreyev's abstractions come close to the manner of the symbolists. The story then returns to a fairly straightforward plot. A wealthy Roman sculptor who hears about Lazarus, out of curiosity deliberately meets his gaze, but loses all his creativity as a result. In the final episode the emperor Augustus summons Lazarus, and tells him that he has no place among the living. Augustus survives the encounter with Lazarus' eyes and is not engulfed by 'the black womb of the Infinite' because he resolutely thinks of his responsibility to his subjects as he looks at Lazarus. Andreyev seems to say in this story that a preoccupation with death can prevent men from living fully, and that few are strong enough to resist. The story is undeniably gloomy, and Gorky naturally found it alien to his way of thinking.

Andreyev was still interested in a biblical theme when he started his next story, *Judas Iscariot*. In February 1907, when he was still deeply depressed by the death of Alexandra, he took up writing again and found it did help to relieve his pain. He told his son 'I wrote the first forty pages without knowing what I was writing, and constantly saw the face of your mother. I threw away these pages and only then could I write'. A contemporary poem on

Judas was one of the original inspirations of the story, which Andreyev planned to put it in the next *Fakely* almanac. However, the writing was postponed until after Alexandra's death, when Andreyev was re-united with Gorky for a time—they had been apart for two years. Under Gorky's influence Andreyev broke off his collaboration with the symbolists. Chulkov, the editor of *Fakely*, wrote in his memoirs that Andreyev always felt unsure of himself amongst the symbolist writers, as he didn't have their assurance in literature or their cultural background. Chulkov complained that Andreyev used to prefer to read adventure stories rather than the classics, and that Schopenhauer's philosophy was the only subject he knew thoroughly. *Judas* was eventually published in the next *Znaniye* almanac. The character of Judas had fascinated Andreyev for some time, and he had frequently painted portraits of Christ and Judas on the same canvas, with Judas' face a distorted copy of that of Christ. Thus in the story which describes the crucifixion from Judas' point of view, Judas is presented as a 'double' of Jesus, ambiguously containing both good and evil in himself. Andreyev gives Judas a cleft skull which divides his face into a good and evil half. *Judas Iscariot* is a more complex and dramatic story than *Lazarus*, and less sombre in tone, for Judas is an active hero and Andreyev does give an original interpretation of Judas' role in the crucifixion. Judas is always treated by the other disciples as an outsider. He is introduced in the story as a man of established bad reputation, but Andreyev questions the automatic labelling of Judas as a traitor. Once having joined the disciples, Judas strives to be accepted, but they are repelled by his unpleasant appearance, his lying and ingratiating personality. Most of all Judas wants to be recognised by Jesus. He would like to be the favourite disciple—but all his efforts to prove his worth are ignored or underrated. In the second half of the story Judas, who now seems superior in intelligence and bravery, takes his revenge on Christ and the disciples. Having arranged to betray Jesus, he gives plenty of warning of the danger, and up to the last moment hopes that people will see their mistake in crucifying Jesus. The failure of any one to act seems to confirm Judas' view that all men are basically evil. Judas' dramatic suicide, hanging himself on a tree which looks over Jerusalem, is a positive gesture of revolt and defiance.

The most interesting part of Judas' characterisation is his rebellion against Jesus. He is a traitor, but paradoxically his treachery seems justified. He rebels because Jesus, the abstraction of truth and goodness personified, does not recognise him. Andreyev presents Judas as a selfish, egotistic man, but he is more complex than earlier heroes, because of the duality of his personality. In an important scene after the crucifixion Judas flings the thirty pieces of silver at the feet of the high priests and Andreyev describes how Judas' face drops its mask, 'the pretence of a lifetime,' and become Christlike, direct and truthful. Judas is obsessed by the fear that people are constantly deceiving him—a theme which Andreyev always treats with some passion, as if it has a very personal significance. The theme of treachery was topical in 1907 after the failure of the revolution, when many intellectuals felt acute despair that autocracy had regained the ascendancy. Alexander Blok found the story very powerfully written and greatly admired it.

Andreyev soon became restless on Capri, and began to quarrel more and more frequently with Gorky, so he decided to take the risk of going back to Russia in the spring of 1907. It was possible that he could have been arrested for his political activities in Finland, but his journey to Moscow and then to St. Petersburg was unhindered. Andreyev now decided that he would prefer to live outside the city, and soon was planning to build his own house some 40 miles north of St. Petersburg, in an isolated spot near the sea. As this took over a year to build, Andreyev moved into a flat in the city, feeling restless and unhappy. He was drinking heavily and still missed Alexandra very painfully, unconsoled by several brief love affairs.

In September 1907 Andreyev finished *Darkness*, a story which so offended Gorky that relations between the two men were broken off for several years. Andreyev took a factual episode about a revolutionary who had sheltered from the police in a brothel, and found time to give the prostitute who concealed him a sermon about her way of life. Naturally she slapped his face. Gorky felt that Andreyev's version distorted the incident and degraded the revolutionary. Andreyev himself said in 1914, perhaps in order to assert his independence from Gorky, that he regarded the story as the best one he had ever written. He complicated the story by making his 26 year old terrorist Aleksei so dedicated to the cause that he has never before had any sexual experience. As a result the necessity of hiding in a brothel creates a much more emotionally charged situation. Aleksei imagines that he is totally unselfish, ready to die for his ideals, but Lyuba (the prostitute) gradually changes his outlook. She asks him why he has the right to be good when she is considered bad. Aleksei's rigid ideas are suddenly altered: 'His life fell apart like a badly glued together box'. Now Aleksei tries to identify with his squalid surroundings, gives up his revolver, gets drunk, and surrenders to the police the following morning. His new philosophy is 'It is shameful to be good'—that is, to be good in the restricted, selfish way he had understood it in the past. Although Aleksei gives up as a revolutionary, he does inspire Lyuba with ambition to become one herself, and the story is not as negative as Gorky judged it.

Andreyev's restlessness and depression in St. Petersburg, and his lifelong dislike of the city and crowds, are combined in another story, *The Curse of the Beast*, dedicated to Alexandra. The narrator is a lonely man, who feels menaced by the city. He feels he is losing his individuality among the masses of people who dress alike, buy the same products and live in houses like coffins. He is appalled by the spectacle of a thousand people chewing at the same time in a crowded restaurant. To escape from the streets he visits the Zoo, which he sees as the city in miniature. The animals are forced to be as submissive as humans, the eagles are reduced to merely hopping round their cages, and the narrator interprets the groan of an elderly seal as a curse, a rebuke to mankind. 'He stood in his dirty pond, in the centre of the huge city and cursed with his animal curse the city, and people, the earth and the sky'.

The spring of 1908 saw the writing of Andreyev's finest story, *The Story of Seven who were Hanged*. After breaking with *Znaniye* the previous summer, Andreyev had to find a new publisher for his stories. He was offered a post as editor on the symbolist journal *Zolotoye Runo* (*The Golden Fleece*), but rejected it, and took up another offer to join a newly formed publishing house *Shipovnik* (*The Wild Rose*). *Shipovnik* was not committed specifically to either realism or symbolism and published work by a wide variety of writers, and therefore suited Andreyev although he never became very closely involved with the enterprise. One stimulus to write *The Story of Seven who were Hanged* was the reading of a pamphlet by Tolstoy, *I Cannot Be Silent*, which protested about the death penalty. In his new story Andreyev described the experiences of seven people under sentence of death. The death penalty was being used fairly often in 1908 in the aftermath of the revolution and Andreyev knew a little about the subject—he had talked to people who had met condemned men in prison, and he had obtained the notes of a political prisoner awaiting execution. (He did not read these until he had finished the story, but then checked them and was pleased to find that the tone was right.) One evening in April Andreyev read the story aloud to some friends in his flat, still continuing the custom of the Wednesday circle days. It had a tremendous effect upon the listeners, as Andreyev had managed to capture the horror of capital punishment most movingly. Tolstoy, to whom it was dedicated, wrote to congratulate Andreyev. It was a story which could please both the realists and those who liked Andreyev's mystical tendencies. (Gorky, perhaps annoyed that *Znaniye* did not have the chance of publishing the story, attacked it because the past lives of revolutionaries were not made sufficiently significant.) However, the protest against the inhumanity of the death penalty is clear, as is Andreyev's concern with the fate of each person facing death alone. The story was enormously successful, 23,000 copies of the *Shipovnik* almanac sold out in a few days. Between 1909 and 1911 the story was printed more than 15 times in about 100,000 copies, and it was translated into several languages and sold well abroad.

The Story of Seven who were Hanged is divided into twelve short chapters, each of which is given a heading, explaining Andreyev's intentions. 'There is no death' and 'Terrible loneliness' are two which sum up the different attitudes of two of the condemned revolutionaries. The story opens by explaining that an important minister is in danger of being assassinated. This introduces one of the themes of the story, that death is much more frightening when the precise hour of it is known. The phrase, 'at one o'clock, your Excellency' is repeated twelve times in the first chapter, as if the minister has himself been sentenced to death, and he is no less lonely in his fear than the revolutionaries will be later. Their arrest reprieves the minister, but now the agony of his would-be assassins begins. As well as the five young intellectuals, two more men are in the condemned cells, and Andreyev's portraits of them are among the best passages in the story. The first is an Estonian worker, a man of limited intelligence, scarcely able to speak Russian. After years of an oppressed existence he suddenly rebelled, murdered his employer and raped the employer's wife. Andreyev shows the Estonian's response to death as a primitive terror. His simple mind can hardly grasp the fact that he is to lose his life and he sinks into passivity during the waiting period. The second ordinary criminal is a lively man from Orel, a natural brigand, nicknamed 'the gypsy'. His mind is almost too active, and he is continually hoping to be able to escape. Both these men howl like animals when they realise death is inevitable, the knowledge having a disintegrating effect on their personalities.

One chapter, 'Kiss and be Silent', which Andreyev found difficult to write, is a restrained account of the parting of two of the young men with their parents, and effectively increases the reader's sympathy. The remaining chapters then show how the five revolutionaries individually react to their imminent death. Two girls among them find it easier to contemplate as they are less self-preoccupied than the men, and they have a genuine altruistic love for mankind. Of the young men, one, Sergei is a 'physical' type, conscious of his strong body, who meticulously performs Müller's gymnastic exercises in prison to keep himself 'fit for death', until his body refuses, registering the fear that his mind had held at bay. The fourth, Vasily, as a more self-centred intellectual type suffers most. The most interesting and intelligent character is Verner. As Andreyev first presents him he seems a coldly intellectual type, proud of his self control. At the trial he is mentally working out a chess problem: 'when he heard the death sentence, not one piece moved on the imaginary board'. Significantly, however, Andreyev calls the chapter which describes Verner's last moments, 'The walls collapse', reminding us of earlier stories where the characters remained imprisoned by the 'walls' of their minds. Verner just before death experiences a sense of joy and identification with the whole of mankind. His limiting selfishness and pride collapses, and he feels free, as if there are no walls to the cell or to his personality. During their last hours the condemned are reunited on their way to the place of execution and Werner helps everyone by his new-found love of mankind. This experience of harmony is an unparalleled moment of optimism in Andreyev's fiction. The closing scenes of the story describe the arrangements for hanging the seven, and give scope for Andreyev to attack ironically the care taken by the authorities to ensure that the hanging is carried out according to the rules. Some critics objected to the naturalistic details at the end of the story, a description of the mutilated corpses, but this is restrained and does not lessen the effectiveness of the protest against capital punishment.

The popularity of the story was such that it could even be said to have had an indirect influence on world history. Andreyev's work was admired and translated by a school-teacher and journalist who lived in Sarajevo, Danilo Ilić. Ilić was associated with Serbian revolutionaries, whose ambition it was to free Bosnia from Austro-Hungarian domination. Gavrilo Princip, who was to assassinate the Archduke Franz Ferdinand on 28th June 1914 lodged with Ilić for a few months beforehand. In May 1914 Ilić wrote an article about Andreyev, placing him above all other contemporary Russian writers. He regarded *The Story of Seven*

Who were Hanged as Andreyev's best work. Ilić was uncertain about assassination as a political weapon, and found Andreyev's story a profound stimulus, emotionally and intellectually. By June 1914 Ilić had agreed to take part in the assassination plot, and it was he who worked out where the conspirators should stand. Thus Andreyev indirectly may have affected one of the events leading to the outbreak of the First World War.

Chapter V

The dramatist

1905 marks a new stage in Andreyev's literary career, when he began to write plays. By November 1906 Gorky was writing enthusiastically about Andreyev's experimental play *The Life of Man*: 'Were I a critic I would write an article about you beginning like this, "There's no doubt in my mind that Leonid Andreyev is at present the most interesting writer in Europe and America. Every new work of his is a significant step forward in form and content along a new and free road, but he hurries too much, and his steps are uneven."' From now on Andreyev began to put more and more of his creative effort into drama, although he continued to write stories, and completed a short novel in 1911. Andreyev regarded his plays with great seriousness, and even saw himself as Chekhov's successor in the Russian theatre.

Once embarked on play writing Andreyev proceeded to write with great speed, never short of ideas. Ibsen used to take about two years to complete a play during his maturity as a dramatist, and Chekhov's four major plays appeared over a period of ten years. Andreyev, on the other hand, finished no less than 20 full length plays between 1905 and 1916, and also 8 shorter pieces. During this period he was of course still writing stories, some of considerable length. Most of Andreyev's plays depended on topicality for their success—a topicality of subject matter, or of dramatic theory and technique, for the theatre was going through a time of change during this period. Plays written at such speed lacked the polish, originality and careful construction of masterpieces, and consequently few of them have been performed since Andreyev's death.

Andreyev set out on his career as a dramatist in 1905 with Gorky's support. Inspired by reading a popular work, *Astronomical Evenings*, by H. Klein, Andreyev conceived the idea for a play about an astronomer. Gorky was also interested in the subject, and in 1904 the two men discussed writing a joint version. This never materialised, probably because they could not agree on the treatment of the idea and in any case Gorky's involvement in revolutionary activity separated them by the end of that year. Andreyev started writing his version, *To the Stars*, towards the end of 1905, transferring the setting he had discussed with Gorky the previous year from Russia to an unnamed Western European country, but adding some topical events of the revolution to the original scheme. (Gorky completed his play *Children of the Sun* in prison in 1905.) Andreyev decided to send *To The Stars* direct to the manager of the famous Moscow Art Theatre, Nemirovich-Danchenko. The latter had founded the theatre in 1898 together with Stanislavsky, and Andreyev had regularly visited their productions. Nemirovich-Danchenko promised to stage it, but the censor rejected the play because of its political content, and it was not performed in Russia for another two years. Andreyev did, however, have the satisfaction of seeing it performed in Vienna at a new left-wing theatre, where it was highly successful. The immediate acceptance of an author's first play was remarkable, especially as Andreyev had not spent a great deal of time studying technique. He was undoubtedly helped by his frequent visits to the theatre over a period of many years, familiarity with contemporary playwrights, and his own reputation as a prose writer. *To the Stars* was also very topical, since it posed the question 'Is revolutionary activity worth while?', which was of burning interest in 1906.

The first plot of *To the Stars*, the life of an astronomer living in a world of trivialities, inspired by the majesty of the universe to rise above his vulgar surroundings, was extended to include characters taking part in the revolution.

The astronomer in Andreyev's play, Ternovsky, lives half way up a mountain, somewhere in Europe, withdrawn from the world and its cares. In the first act his isolation is emphasised by the blizzards which literally cut off the observatory from the bloody events of the revolution in Russia. The play depends on the debate between Ternovsky, the dedicated scientist, and his children, who are taking part in the revolution. When Ternovsky's daughter Anna brings the news that her brother has been arrested, he replies, 'Do people still kill each other there? Are there still prisons there?', showing his indifference to the world of political events. Anna attacks his attitude, 'I'm not against science, but against scientists who make science a pretext to get out of social responsibilities'. Ternovsky argues that man is so insignificant compared to events in the universe that one cannot be concerned about the fate of individuals. The same debate is also echoed by two other characters in the play, Ternovsky's assistant Pollak, a cold young scientist, and a worker, Treich, who is inspired by the romance of the revolution. As the play continues and battered victims of the revolution crawl back to the mountain refuge, it is clear that Andreyev's sympathies are more with the astronomer. Ternovsky criticises people who think only about their own life and death and consequently live in a state of fear. If you can only hear the 'voice of the stars', he suggests, you will become the 'son of eternity'. In the final act Ternovsky's daughter-in-law Marusya brings the news that her husband has gone mad in prison. Marusya, too, cannot accept Ternovsky's indifference to life on earth, and says that the stars (representing higher aspirations) are alien to her. Ternovsky insists that 'There is no death for mankind, no death for the son of eternity'. Man is immortal as part of the whole of life, and his personality lives on after death, embodied in everyone who has ever known him. Ternovsky's philosophy is very similar to that of Verner in *The Seven who were Hanged*. However, in the final act Marusya is given a chance to put forward her ideas and suggests that Ternovsky's ideas may be lacking in essential humanity.

Stimulated by the success of *To the Stars*, it was not long before Andreyev completed his second play *Savva*. This too is written in a fairly traditional form, and as in nearly all Andreyev's plays is motivated by a conflict of ideas, rather than one of emotion or personality. Andreyev had first thought about the subject matter in 1902, and the events closely followed an episode reported to have taken place a few years previously. An inventor tried to combat religious superstition by blowing up an icon

95

which was reputed to perform miracles. In Andreyev's play the inventor has become Savva, a young man who wants to build a new world, replacing the old one which is tainted by the restrictive nature of society. Savva would like to destroy literature, art and cities, and puts forward the same sort of ideas that Andreyev used in *Thus it was* or *The Curse of the Beast*, about the innate servility of man and his tendency to build prisons for himself. An argument in favour of the miraculous icon is put forward by Savva's sister, Lipa. The icon does bring some sort of joy to people who are suffering. Savva's revolt fails, and he is betrayed in his plans to destroy the icon, because no one supports his selfish aims. Finally an angry crowd murders him. In this play Andreyev expresses indirectly his own fear of too much violence in any revolutionary activity. Savva's self-centred motives are purely destructive, and will not achieve any results in liberating man from himself.

The play that gained Andreyev most publicity and fame in his life time was *The Life of Man*, although it has suffered the fate of the other plays and is never staged to-day. Andreyev wrote the play in October 1906 in a concentrated burst of work which lasted twelve days. Just as he had tried to evolve a new form of story for *The Red Laugh*, so with *The Life of Man* Andreyev tried to reform the traditional pattern of plays. The play is allegorical, and the characters are generalisations of types, called only Man, Man's wife or Someone in Grey, supported by groups of people like a chorus, such as 'old women' or 'friends of Man'. The term *act* is replaced by *picture*, indicating Andreyev's wish to see each stage in the play as a kind of animated picture. *The Life of Man* is based on mediaeval representations of the stages in man's life, and Gorky commented, 'It seems to me that you have taken the forms of the old mystery, but have discarded the mystery heroes, with extremely interesting and original results'. Andreyev said that the idea had come to him from seeing Dürer's woodcuts in Germany, and the stage directions make it clear that each act is another picture, framed by a large room.

Man goes through five stages of life in the play, and a mysterious omniscient figure, Someone in Grey, accompanies him, representing his inevitable destiny. Someone in Grey stands in the corner of the stage holding a candle, which burns down a little more in each act. The whole emphasis of the play is on man's helplessness to change his predetermined path through life. The first picture has a predominantly black and grey colour scheme, representing the pain of birth, but in the second,— youth—the background is pink, and there are flowers and bright clothes symbolising hope.

The third picture, the most resplendent (influenced by a Goya painting) depicts a ball, but already there is less colour as Man ages, and Andreyev includes in the stage directions some bars of music composed by himself. These, he instructs, are to be played deliberately out of time. The fourth and fifth pictures, Man's old age and death, take place against a sombre backcloth, as the candle burns further down. Man does display some defiance of fate—he curses it when his son dies but he cannot alter his predestined career, predicted in the prologue by Someone in Grey. The death scene is set in a tavern (this was changed in a later version of the play) with a chorus of drunkards, one of whom objects to the inevitability of death: 'I am firmly convinced that there is an error here. A straight line that presents the form of a closed circle is simply ridiculous'. The foreshadowing of death throughout the play does give the static scenes of stages in man's life dramatic tension. The only 'event' is the premature death of Man's son.

When the play was finished Andreyev sent it to Russia, one copy to his friend Teleshov, asking that it should be read out at a 'Wednesday Circle' meeting, a second copy to the editor of the symbolist journal *Fakely*, and a third to Nemirovich-Danchenko. Andreyev wanted to hear the opinion of different people about the new dramatic form he believed he had invented. In the event the play was first published in the middle of the road *Shipovnik* almanac, but its stage production was the most sensational part of its history. The theatre in Russia, just as much as literature, had been affected by new movements in art at the turn of the century. Bryusov, the leader of the decadent writers, had stated in 1902 that naturalism in the theatre was outdated, and that real life could not be portrayed on the stage any more. Producers began to think in terms of stylised versions of plays, where the actors were to display as little emotion as possible. Each production was designed to concentrate on a particular idea or mood. Vsevolod Meyerhold, an actor turned director, one of the keenest experimenters in non-realistic drama, found that *The Life of Man* almost exactly complied with his ideas at the time, and staged it in St. Petersburg in February 1907, very shortly after its completion. In fact Meyerhold did not pay too much attention to Andreyev's directions, and produced something very much in accordance with his own new theories. The stage was dark much of the time, make up was exaggerated and there was hardly any scenery. The actor who played Someone in Grey had to read the monologues totally without expression. Andreyev was not entirely in agreement with Meyerhold's interpretation, considering that too much gloominess had been introduced and that Man was insufficiently rebellious. Alexander Blok on the other hand watched a performance of the play from the wings, and was deeply moved by it. Again he spoke of the 'inner chaos' he discerned in Andreyev's writing, and felt that Meyerhold had improved the play. The Moscow Art Theatre had also agreed to stage *The Life of Man*, and later in 1907 Stanislavsky worked out a different interpretation from the St. Petersburg production, although it was still to be in the new anti-naturalistic mood. Andreyev wrote a long letter to Stanislavsky, asking him to bring out the sharp contrasts in the play, to give more weight to Man than to Someone in Grey. Stanislavsky did alter the emphasis, allowing the actors to put much more expression in their voices, and startled his audiences by swathing the stage in black velvet. After successful seasons in the capitals the play was later staged in several provincial towns, and began to be heckled by members of The Black Hundreds, who regarded it as blasphemous. The fact that after these disturbances the play was subsequently banned in several major cities made it all the more popular. The critics were enthusiastic, and Andreyev was awarded a literary prize for *The Life of Man* in December 1907, marking his success as a dramatist.

Andreyev's next two plays, both written in 1907, were allegorical in manner, *The Black Masks* and *Tsar Hunger*. In the first of these it seems as if Andreyev was working to a specification illustrating another of the dramatic theories of the day. Certain playwrights were interested in the presentation of psychological portraits on stage. A contemporary producer and dramatist, Yevreinov, had worked out the theory of what he called the Monodrama, in which he saw the spectator identifying himself completely with the principle character of the play. There is no record that Andreyev wrote *The Black Masks* with this idea in mind, but Yevreinov welcomed it as one of the few plays to come close to realising the Monodrama. The setting of the play is a splendid mediaeval Italian castle (the play was written when Andreyev was living on Capri.) The main character is the owner of the castle, Lorenzo, Duke of Spadaro. (Gorky in his memoirs complained that lack of attention to detail was typical of Andreyev's writing. Spadaro was a proletarian name—probably suggested to Andreyev by a colourful local fisherman popular with visitors to Capri. Gorky also objected to the historical inaccuracy of St. Bernard dogs in the twelfth century castle.) The play opens with Lorenzo waiting with happy expectancy in his castle, blazing with lights, to receive his guests. They arrive in fancy dress, their faces concealed under close fitting masks. Gradually the mood changes to one of horror, as Lorenzo fails to recognise anyone under their masks, including his servants and his own wife. The masked figures become more and more unpleasant and menacing. The allegory becomes clearer when a stage direction introduces a new, even more grotesque visitor.

'Something formless and shapeless, with many arms and legs crawls in. It speaks with many voices. "We are your thoughts, Lorenzo".
Lorenzo—"What an insolent joke, signori. But you are my guests—I invited you".
The thing—"We are your masters, Lorenzo. This castle is ours"'.

The castle is Lorenzo's mind, and he has tried to understand what is inside. Lorenzo even meets his own double and kills him, as in Poe's story, *William Wilson*. After he has killed his double, figures in black masks crowd into the castle, representing Lorenzo's madness. In the final act Lorenzo waits for guests in his empty castle, although none will come, and he dies in a fire which destroys the whole building.

The Black Masks puzzled audiences who saw it, as the allegory is more obscure than in *The Life of Man*. More light is thrown on it in the story *My Memoirs*, which was completed the following year. This is an interesting story, written in diary form, with the style well sustained, but it seemed to Gorky to preach a passive attitude to life. The hero is a mathematician (like Verner in *The Story of Seven who were Hanged*) who has been in prison all his life on a suspected murder charge. The prison is another of Andreyev's symbols for the negative restricting role of the intellect. The mathematician, who has the same pride in his logical thinking as Dr. Kerzhentsev in *Thought*, reconciles himself to liking his prison, and ends up by praising the iron bars which keep him in. When eventually freed he sets up his own prison cell and hires a warder, thus revealing his basically servile nature. In *My Memoirs* Andreyev inserts a summary of the plot of *Black Masks*, fitting it into the mathematician's reflections on the difficulty of distinguishing between lies and truth within one's soul. He explains the allegory of *The Black Masks*. 'The castle is the soul; the owner is man; the strange masks are those forces which are active in man's soul, whose secret being he can never understand'. It is now clear that in the play Lorenzo was trying to achieve the impossible by guessing the identity of his guests. The intellect, according to Andreyev, is too limited to comprehend the mysteries of life.

The second allegorical play which Andreyev wrote in 1907, *Tsar Hunger*, was to be a sequel to *The Life of Man*. A cycle of five plays of this type were originally planned, but *King Hunger* was the last to be completed. Like *The Life of Man* its subject matter is abstract, and all characters are reduced to generalised types. *Tsar Hunger* is the embodiment of a force which makes men rebel; he incites workers to rebel against their master, and the poor to destroy the wealthy. The conclusions seem pessimistic —man is out for himself, whatever class he belongs to, and will destroy culture in order to achieve power. Despite the fact that the play was well constructed, it did not have the success of *The Life of Man*, and Andreyev's next play showed a return to realism. *The Days of Our Life* (1908) draws on Andreyev's memories of student days for its subject matter, and in fact he had worked out the details in an early manuscript ten years previously. Andreyev did not regard the play as particularly significant, probably because it expounds few abstract ideas about life, and sent it to *Znaniye* for publication. Andreyev worked on it at the same time as *Black Masks*, and wrote to Nemirovich-Danchenko that the latter play would be much more suitable for the Moscow Art Theatre. A well known theatre critic A. R. Kugel received a copy of *The Days of Our Life* and later Andreyev wrote to him, 'I'm glad you like the play, although I regard it as a trifle. Perhaps it will go down well, now that Russians are unmasking themselves, and our respected symbolists are turning into respected realists. The king is dead, long live the king. In case of catastrophes with the censor, all the military characters can be retired. Let them be ensigns of the reserve'. The reference to symbolists shows Andreyev's awareness of the growing challenge to the symbolist movement as the mood in Russia changed, and of the declining popularity of theatrical experiments. *The Days of our Life* was first performed in St. Petersburg in November 1908, and ran for 74 performances, followed by a season in Moscow and the provinces. The play is full of action and lively dialogue. A group of students enjoy life despite their appalling poverty. One of them, Kolya, is in love. His eighteen year old girl friend is being forced into prostitution by her mother, and the play deals with Kolya's struggle to reconcile his youthful idealism with the unpleasant facts of life. It was highly successful and accessible to a far wider audience than *The Black Mvsks*, since it dealt in a straightforward way with social problems, and of all Andreyev's plays it lasted longest in Russian theatre repertoires—performances were given up to 1938.

Andreyev's last attempt to write a modernistic play was a compromise between realism and allegory, *Anathema*. It was finished by the end of 1908, and Nemirovich–Danchenko accepted it for the Art Theatre. The censor's objections were overcome fairly quickly—a few minor alterations had to be made—and rehearsals were started in February 1909. Nemirovich–Danchenko, who saw it as a realistic tragedy, had several heated arguments with Andreyev about the interpretation of the play, and the two men nearly came to blows on more than one occasion during the 89 rehearsals. Nemirovich–Danchenko saw it as a play dealing with poverty, whereas Andreyev described it as dedicated to 'the problem of man's attainment of immortality'. In *Anathema*, said Andreyev, this problem is solved by love. The play begins with a prologue in a mythical setting. The curtain rises to show iron gates 'tightly closed', half way up a mountain and beyond them, we are told, is the 'supreme wisdom of the universe'. Anathema (or Satan), 'someone accursed', cannot get past the gates, and to show his defiance of heaven he decides to meddle in events on earth. Anathema brings unexpected wealth to a poor Jew, David Leizer, and suggests that he can gain immortality by giving away his money. David does this, and when there is no money left the crowd turn against him and stone him to death as Anathema expects. Like Judas Iscariot in Andreyev's story he has no faith in human nature.

However, in the final scene the guardian of the gates explains to Anathema that David did gain immortality, for he died thinking of others. The play was received with moderate enthusiasm, mainly due to the skill of the actor who played Anathema. Andreyev sent a copy of the play to Tolstoy, now in the last year of his life, who read the first four pages of the prologue and dismissed it as pretentious nonsense. *Anathema* was also produced in St. Petersburg, rather less successfully, for it was acted in the expressionless style now rapidly going out of fashion, and the play seemed very wooden. *Anathema* gained more fame in 1910, when a bishop preached a sermon condemning it as evil. The censor looked at it again, and further performances were banned after pressure from the church. Before the ban Andreyev had started making notes on a film version, and for three years a film producer called Drankov tried to get permission to make it, but without success.

In November 1911 Andreyev completed his first *Letter on the Theatre* (a second followed a year later), an attempt to produce his own theory of drama and provide a basis for his further play writing. Andreyev regretted that 'healthy' realism had taken over in the theatre, and thought that this had led to a lowering of standards, scathingly commenting that in order to clear the air of the symbolist dramatist Maeterlinck, the nineteenth century realist Ostrovsky was being revived on the Russian stage. The cinema appealed to Andreyev, as he thought it could now take over from the theatre the role of depicting action and realistic scenery. Andreyev commented that the silent screen was also an advantage, as it meant that films could be international. He thought that the theatre of the future should describe struggles going on in the mind of the protagonist, rather than external events. He called the old theatre the 'theatre of make-believe', whereas the new was to be the 'theatre of panpsyche and of truth'—psychology was the most important factor. Andreyev's theories owe something to those of Maeterlinck, who undoubtedly influenced his plays. Maeterlinck had said in *The Treasure of The Humble* (1897) that the portrayal of violent actions on stage was out of date. He called for a static theatre: 'The beauty and greatness of tragedies are found not in actions but in words'. By 1910 a new quest for tragedy in the Russian theatre was fashionable. Tragic plays, it was felt, would best inspire the audience. Blok had expressed this mood when he reviewed Judas Iscariot: 'Andreyev is on the edge of tragedy, which we are all waiting and longing for'. Moreover, Andreyev was certainly familiar with Schopenhauer's view of tragedy as the highest form of drama. 'In it the misery of existence is brought before us and the final outcome is here the vanity of all human striving'. Andreyev was now well equipped with theories to guide him, but in practice his later plays did not differ very greatly in their basic ideas from earlier works.

After 1910 the critics began to pay less attention to Andreyev's new plays, although most were performed in Russia. He followed his own theories to a certain extent, writing two plays which were conceived as tragedies, *The Ocean* (1911) and *Samson in Chains* (1915), both in a historical setting. In several others he concentrated on the psychology of the main character, using a background of middle class family life. One of the most interesting of these is *Yekaterina Ivanovna* (1912), in which the heroine is gradually corrupted by the influence of those around her. Perhaps the best known of Andreyev's later plays outside Russia is *He who gets Slapped*. In this play abstract ideas and realism blend successfully and there is some real dramatic tension. Andreyev wrote *He who gets Slapped* in the summer of 1915, when he was suffering from almost continuous headaches and heart trouble, but once he started on the play his illnesses seemed to disappear and he completed it in a month. The setting for this play is a circus, a world where people live by intuition and emotion, whereas the outside world represents cold, intellectual life. One day an unknown man who refuses to give his name appears, the 'He' of the title, asking to join the circus as a clown. 'He' has rejected the outside world because he has been deceived by his wife, and his ideas have been stolen by a friend and published in a successful book. 'He' falls in love with Consuella, one of the circus artistes, who is a classically beautiful woman. She has had no education to spoil her nature, and Andreyev explained that she is a tragic figure because her divine soul is imprisoned in the everyday world. On stage 'He' as the clown plays the part of a pompous intellectual who gets slapped continuously, and thus amuses the audience. When Consuella seems to be fated to marry a wealthy but physically repulsive Baron, 'He' poisons her, perhaps symbolising the fact that intellect destroys the things it most wants, in this case true beauty. The play was popular, as it could be enjoyed without an understanding of Andreyev's underlying ideas, and it went on being performed in Russia up to 1922. A film version was made in 1916, and the play was used as the basis of an opera, *Pantaloon*, by the American composer Robert Varda (1956).

Andreyev's one-act plays are usually less serious in intention and are more satirical, in the style of his journalism. *Love Thy Neighbour* (1908) is an early attack on the immorality of advertising, and of the ease with which people's love of sensation can be exploited. A man is clinging precariously to a cliff face, and it is obvious that he will fall soon. Meanwhile a crowd of tourists has collected below, the press arrives and so do priests of more than one faith. Then it turns out that the man has been paid for the stunt by the owner of the café at the foot of the cliff. The tourists are disappointed that they have wasted film in their cameras. One of Andreyev's last short plays, *Requiem*, was, however, entirely serious. The setting of the play is itself a theatre, but one deprived of all life; the spectators are mock wooden figures, the actors are like corpses and the whole building is dark and empty. Here some of Andreyev's bitterness at the failure of his later plays may be felt. He had thought he had important things to say, which could best be expressed by plays of the type of *The Life of Man*, and the rejection of these was hard to accept.

Chapter VI

Finland

By the spring of 1908 Andreyev's new house near the village of Vammelsuu in Finland was ready, and the family moved in. It was a large wooden building with fifteen rooms, situated in a fairly remote area where other St. Petersburg families would only spend the summer months. Newspaper reports suggested that the house was 'menacing and gloomy', or 'the castle of death', seeing it as an example of one of the many images of sinister buildings in Andreyev's fiction. These reports were exaggerated, but there is no doubt that Andreyev in designing the house incorporated features from his imaginary world. Andreyev's son Vadim recalled how the wooden exterior darkened in time, and did give a sombre impression. Inside, vastness was the keynote—rooms were spacious, and the furniture massive, specially built in *art nouveau* style to Andreyev's specification. There were huge sofas, and yards of heavy curtains, which made the interior dark, despite the many windows. Andreyev's own study contained a desk of gigantic proportions and had a balcony where he liked to observe the sunrise after a night's work. The walls were hung with copies of Goya's paintings, made by Andreyev himself. A major disadvantage of the house was that it was not possible to heat it adequately in the coldest winter months. Andreyev's mother settled in to yet another new home, and was soon back to her task of making endless glasses of tea. While the house was being built Andreyev took a great deal of interest in the construction work, spending hours discussing details with the workers and helping where he could. (One of his hands was scarred and not fully efficient because of a childhood accident — he had fallen on a broken bottle while skating.) Once the house was ready Andreyev set to work on the garden, and planted dozens of trees, but the soil was poor and most of these died.

Two rooms in the house were planned as nurseries, and it was not long before Andreyev remarried. Early in 1908 he had advertised for a secretary, but there were so many replies that he pushed them aside in despair, and took on a young lady recommended by his friend the writer and critic, Kornei Chukovsky. Her name was Anna Denisevich, and not long afterwards Andreyev proposed marriage. While this second marriage did not recapture the idyllic happiness of the first, it was a reasonably stable and pleasant relationship. Anna was very devoted to her husband, bore him three children, typed out much of his later work as he dictated it, and nursed him during the frequent periods of ill health of his last years. She also tolerated his occasional love affairs very well. In January 1915 Andreyev wrote to a friend 'I live well with Anna, but I have my day dreams about conquests. I would like an affair—I'm still young at heart. I'd like a ballerina, or a chaste young girl'.

The new house seemed to be designed to favour creative work, and Vadim Andreyev recalled how everyone in it, including one of the servants, was inspired to write or paint. Yet there was a sense of impermanence and unreality, and it is striking how Andreyev himself never recaptured in his huge well-furnished study the inspiration of earlier restless years. Once he had settled in to the house, Andreyev's fame very slowly began to slip away, and the critics became gradually more hostile. For a time Andreyev seemed determined to get the most out of life. The house was always full of relatives and guests, and sometimes these overflowed into neighbouring *dachas*. Andreyev's entertainment was lavish—magnificent picnics in summer which took hours to arrange, and skiing for everyone in the winter. Andreyev liked noise and clamour around him, perhaps to stifle his own depression. People were essential to him, and he was upset if no weekend visitors from St. Petersburg arrived. He would then pick up the telephone and ask friends to come and discuss something of the utmost importance, which could not be mentioned in public. The guests once they had hurried to Andreyev's house would find that the call had simply been a ruse. Andreyev's habit of writing or talking all night had not changed, although he was now increasingly troubled by severe headaches, bad enough at times to make him fear he was going blind. His heart was also not functioning properly, but this didn't prevent him from being physically active.

In Finland Andreyev enthusiastically resumed all his hobbies, characteristically devoting himself to one thing at a time with enormous energy and enjoyment. He cultivated the garden, took numerous photographs and developed them himself, and painted furiously. His greatest pleasure was sailing, and he eventually acquired a boat built according to his own design. In this Andreyev used to set off alone and stay away for weeks sailing round the Finnish coast. He acquired a lot of equipment, and learnt all the correct nautical terminology. Generally the press grew more hostile to Andreyev in the last decade of his life, and his name appeared in the papers frequently, usually in totally inaccurate accounts of disorderly life at his home. The Finnish house placed a considerable strain upon his finances, and although Andreyev was still earning large amounts from his current writing and reprints of earlier work, his lavish hospitality and extravagant way of life was barely covered by his income. There was a gradual deterioration in his position.

From 1908 Andreyev was busy turning out at least two plays each year, and a few short stories as well. The most ambitious prose work he completed in Finland was the novel *Sashka Zhegulev*, which he first drafted while he was on Capri. This novel was based on the actual adventures of a revolutionary who became a bandit in the unsettled period of the 1905 revolution. Andreyev's hero Sashka, after a sheltered middle-class upbringing, breaks out to become a revolutionary, dedicated and ready to sacrifice himself to the cause. After tasting blood in terrorist activities, Sashka becomes a bandit, and for a time creates havoc, before he is killed ignominiously. The novel, showing some influence of Dostoyevsky in its style and construction, also includes a number of typically Andreyevan themes, but it is of uneven quality, and Sashka's transformation seems insufficiently motivated. Gorky later wrote about it, 'The novel is written, I should say, with a superfluous emphasis, and is over-burdened with psychology, but it is a correct and true portrait of one of those Russian dreamers who believe that the evil of life can be conquered by the same power of evil'. A more effective story written in 1911 is *Rest*. An elderly bureaucrat is dying, and is visited by a devil, who offers him the choice between an afterlife in hell, or oblivion. The devil is bored with his job and looks scruffy—the official notices the mud on his fur with distaste. 'The devil placed a piece of paper before the official. It was rather dirty, and more like a hand-kerchief than such an important document. "Here" he indicated with his talon. "No, no, not there. Here if you want to go to hell. Here if you want death"'. The choice is so difficult that the old mans signs with his eyes shut, and is agonised to find he has opted for death.

The outbreak of war in 1914 was a new stimulus to Andreyev, now in declining health, and dispirited by his diminishing fame. He felt he had a new mission to express his ideas about Russia. His response once Russia entered the war, unlike 1904 when he wrote *The Red Laugh*, was not pacificism, but fierce patriotism. This patriotism was shared by many people at the beginning of the war, but soon it turned to despair and criticism of the appalling inefficiency of Nicholas II's ministers and army. (Patrio-tism and anti-German feeling led to the re-naming of St. Petersburg as Petrograd.) However, Andreyev's love of Russia outweighed all other considerations and he remained loyal to government policy, despite disillusionments, being overjoyed by victories and plunged into despair by defeats. War also had a greater significance for him now—it was a purifying force which could change the corrupt society he had so often attacked in his writings, and it seemed part of the cosmic catastrophe which the symbolists had expected for so long. Andreyev's immediate response was a play, based on the invasion of Belgium *The King, Law and Liberty*, completed in October 1914, but art in this play took second place to propaganda. In 1915 *The Yoke of War*, an account of the first year of war in Petrograd written in diary form by a citizen, shows some of Andreyev's disappointment that the war did not purge men's souls, but in fact led to profiteering and greater corruption. Yet he still advocates patriotism and says that Russia must come first.

Andreyev would probably have taken a more active part in the war if his health had not prevented him. He was now looking much older, his face was heavily lined, and he had acquired a stoop. Despite illness in 1916 he undertook to edit the literary section in a new paper *Russkaya Volya* financed by right wing capitalist interests. Andreyev was strongly criticised by other writers for joining the paper, and

119

Gorky, Korolenko and Blok refused to contribute to it. However, Andreyev genuinely believed it would be fairly progressive, and also desperately needed the financial security it gave him,—a guaranteed 50,000 roubles a year. For a time he plunged himself into the role of an editor, but his poor health and gradual disillusionment with the aims of the paper meant that this was not sustained for long. He was still contributing, however, a year later when the October revolution of 1917 put an end to the paper.

In 1917 the February revolution excited Andreyev for a while and brought him new energy, but soon he returned to a gloomy frame of mind, dominated by his poor health. Vadim Andreyev recalled how he found some relaxation at this time playing with his children, and even went out cycling despite his heart condition, but always lapsed back into a silent mood. The October revolution introduced a period of real hardship for the family, who were now virtually confined to their Finnish house. This was in need of repairs which couldn't be undertaken now, and shortage of fuel meant that most of the rooms had to be closed. Vadim recalled how soup spilt in the dining room froze immediately. Andreyev's last visit to Petrograd was early in 1918, when he went to see his mother, who was ill with pneumonia, despite risk of arrest because of his association with right wing groups in 1917. Andreyev wrote often to his mother, and one of the few letters which have survived dates from this time. In it he recognised how his mother had accompanied him faithfully throughout his life. 'I know good families, where relations are good between parents and children, but I've never found a relationship such as yours and mine'.

From the spring of 1918 the civil war in Russia began to affect the Andreyevs. The 'White' (anti-Bolshevik) forces occupied the area of Finland where they lived, cutting them off from Petrograd. This meant that a period of near starvation began for the family, who were now without any money or resources. In the autumn of that year Andreyev managed to mortgage the house and was then able to move further north to a small town where conditions were a little better. There was more food, but leaving his own home was a deep blow to Andreyev. Now he was a lonely man, having lost contact with his former literary friends, and the only enthusiasm which sustained him was a fierce hatred of the Bolsheviks, who he felt were destroying Russia's culture and moral values. As Andreyev had never lost his conviction that Russia should continue the war, the Bolshevik peace treaty with Germany was an act of treachery in his eyes. Thus in 1919

Andreyev wrote an appeal called *S. O. S.* to the allies, America, Britain and France after they had appeared to compromise and accept the Bolsheviks as the new leaders of Russia. Andreyev's passionate tract asks the allies to come to Russia's aid and drive out the Bolsheviks. Andreyev was actually offered a post as propaganda minister in the projected government of the White General Yudenich, and he travelled to Helsinki to meet officials. He was unfavourably impressed by them and refused but made plans to visit Europe and America on a lecture tour to spread his anti-Bolshevik views. Of course his health was so poor now that there was no question of such a tour—he had had a serious heart attack at the end of 1918. Despite all his suffering Andreyev continued to write, and in 1919 worked on a long story, *Satan's Diary*, using his recollections of a visit to Rome just before the war as the background of this account of another devil who spends some time on earth. War was now coming close to the Andreyevs' home, and in the last month of his life the writer lived through air raids by Bolshevik planes. Andreyev died on 12th September 1919, at the age of 49, from a heart attack. Only a few relatives and friends were present at his modest funeral, and in Russia, shaken by revolution and civil war, his death was almost unnoticed at the time—something which would have been unthinkable ten years previously.

In the diary he kept during the difficult days of 1918, Andreyev in one entry tried to assess his own literary achievement. He asks the question, 'Why did I stop? The first ten years were a line of almost unbroken progress?' The answer he gave, after looking at his failure to live up to the promise of his work up to 1908, is this: 'I betrayed myself. Born to anathematise, I just handed out indulgences'. Andreyev was judging himself severely at this time, for one outstanding feature about all his writing is its seriousness of purpose. This has been ignored in the generally hostile critical judgements made about him since his death, which have alleged that he was an imitative, superficial writer, exploiting his readers by using sensational effects. Tolstoy's remark, 'Andreyev tries to scare us but I am not afraid', has often been quoted to support these views. This is unjust, for Andreyev was always sincere in his attempts to bring home to his readers the dangers he thought they were facing. He chose fantastic or horrible situations and dramatic, hyperbolic language in order to convey his passionately held beliefs to the reader, and he may be considered a precursor of Expressionism. Andreyev may not have been helped by his own popularity, as for years he never experienced the sobering effect of rejected work, so that he was not obliged to revise and perfect his narrative technique. As Gorky said, Andreyev treated his talent 'like a bad rider on a good horse' in his haste to get ideas on to paper. Nevertheless, Andreyev's remarkable imagination, intelligence and sensitivity are clearly discernible in his best works which made him for a decade one of the most popular writers in Russia.

Further reading

Books in English

J. B. Woodward, *Leonid Andreyev: a study*, Oxford, The Clarendon Press, 1969.

A. Kaun, *Leonid Andreyev: a critical study*, New York, 1924. (Currently available in a photocopy by Bell and Howell.)

P. Yershov, *ed. The Letters of Gorky and Andreyev 1899–1912*, New York 1958.

Books in Russian

Kniga o Leonide Andreyeve: vospominaniya. Russian writers on Leonid Andreyev. Berlin, 1922. Reprinted by Prideaux Press, Letchworth, 1970.

Gor'kiy i Leonid Andreyev, neizdannaya perepiska, Literaturnoye nasledstvo, tom 72, Moscow 1965.

L. Afonin, *Leonid Andreyev*, Orel, 1959.

Editions of Andreyev's works

In Russian

No complete edition of Andreyev's works has ever been compiled. The most comprehensive collection can be found in:

Polnoye sobraniye sochineniy, St. Petersburg, 1913, 8 volumes.

Selected stories and plays:

Povesti i rasskazy, Mocsow, 1957.
P'esy, Moscow, 1959.
Selected stories, ed. M. Shotton, with notes and a vocabulary, Bradda Books, Letchworth, 1970.

A new edition of selected stories in two volumes was due to be published in Moscow by the end of 1970.

In English

Numerous plays and stories were translated into English in Andreyev's lifetime and the 1920s. Alexander Kaun's critical study lists plays and stories translated up to 1923. Thirty eight stories in translation included in various collections are listed in the *Short Story Index*, New York, H. W. Wilson Co., 1953.

Two more recent translations are:

Seven that were hanged, and other stories, New York, Random House, 1958.
Twentieth Century Russian Drama, tr. A. R. MacAndrew, New York, 1963. (This includes *He who gets slapped*.)

Contents

Chapter I	Early years	5
Chapter II	Maxim Gorky and the "Wednesday Circle". . . .	23
Chapter III	The Abyss	43
Chapter IV	War and Revolution	63
Chapter V	The Dramatist	91
Chapter VI	Finland	113

INDEX

Andreyev, Alexandra (nee Veligorskaya) 20, 44, 77, 79, 83, 84
Andreyev, Anastasiya 6-8, 14-18, 120, 121
Andreyev, Anna 114, 115
Andreyev, Leonid :
    About the Russian Intellectual 25
    Abyss, The 42, 45-47, 48
    Anathema 105-107
    At the Window 31, 35
    Bargamot and Garaska 25, 26
    Black Masks, The 101-105
    Christians 76, 77
    Curse of the Beast, The 84, 96
    Darkness 83, 84
    Days of Our Life 19, 104, 105
    Deception 39
    Festival, the 32
    Foreigner, The 33
    From a Story which will Not be Finished 73
    Gaudeamus 19
    Grand Slam, The 17, 35
    Governor, The 74-76
    He who gets Slapped 109, 110
    In Springtime 14
    In the Fog 45, 47-48
    Into the Dark Distance 34
    Judas Iscariot 79-82
    King, Law and Liberty, The 119
    Laughter 39

Lazarus 78-80

Letter on the Theatre 107, 108

Life of Man, The 91, 96-100, 102, 104, 111

Life of Vasili Fiveisky, The 56-60

Love Thy Neighbour 111

Marseillaise 73

My Memoirs 102, 103

Ocean, The 109

Once There Lived 36

On the River 31

Peter at the Dacha 30

Red Laugh, The 64-68, 76, 96, 118

Requiem 111

Rest 118

Samson in Chains 109

Sashka Zhegulev 117

Satan's Diary 122

Savva 95, 96

Silence 27, 34

S.O.S. 122

Story of Sergei Petrovich, The 38

Story of Seven who were Hanged, The 85-90, 95 103

Thought 53-56

Thus it was 71-3, 96

To the Stars 92-95

Tsar Hunger 101, 103

Wall, The 40-42

Wild Duck, The 49

Yoke of War, The 119

Andreyev, Nicolai 6-8, 13, 14
Andreyev, Vadim 69, 113, 115
Bergson, H. 53
Blok, A.A. 60, 61, 82, 100, 108, 120
Bryusov, V.Y. 99
Bunin, I.A. 23
Chekhov, A.P. 19, 23, 29, 35, 39, 51, 55, 91
    A Man in a Case 35
    Ward No. 6 37
Chulkov, G.I. 80
Cooper, James Fenimore 9
Courier, The 21, 23-26, 28, 30, 41, 48
Dickens, Charles 9
Dostoyevsky, F.M. 54, 117
    Crime and Punishment 54
Dumas, A. 64
Everybody's Journal 27, 30, 41
Fakely 73, 80, 98
Freud, S. 50
Gorky, Maxim 7, 23, 25-27, 29, 33, 34, 41, 42, 49,
51, 53, 55, 59-61, 65-67, 69, 71, 72, 77, 79, 80,
82-84, 86, 91-93, 97, 117, 120, 124
    Childhood 7
    Old Izergil 35
    The Song of the Stormy Petrel 41
    Man 56
    Children of the Sun 93
Hartman, E. Von 12, 50
Ibsen, H. 49, 91
Ilić, D. 89, 90
Korolenko, V.G. 25, 51, 120

Lynch, James (pseudonym of Leonid Andreyev) 25
Maeterlinck, M. 108
   The Treasure of the Humble 108
Mayne-Reid, T. 9
Meyerhold, V.E. 99, 100
Mikhailovsky, N.K. 42, 55
Mirolyubov, V.S. 27
Moscow Herald 21
Nemirovich-Danchenko, V.I. 93, 98, 104, 106
New Time 45
Nietzsche, F. 38
   Thus Spake Zarathustra 38
Orel Herald 18, 19
Ostrovsky, A.N. 108
Poe, Edgar Allan 9
   The Fall of the House of Usher 59
   William Wilson 102
Pravda 74
Russkaya Volya 119
Schopenhauer, A. 12, 35, 46, 49, 50, 53, 80, 108
   The World as Will and Idea 49
Shalyapin, F.I, 60
Shipovnik 85, 86, 99
Skitalets, S.G. 69
Stanislavsky, K.S. 93, 100
Teleshov, N.D. 27, 98
Tolstoy, Count Dmitri 10
Tolstoy, L.N., 12, 13, 28, 35, 37, 48, 68, 75, 86, 107,
123
   What I Believe 12
   What is Art 28

    The Death of Ivan Il'ich 37
    The Kreutzer Sonata 48
    I Cannot be Silent 85
Tolstoy, Countess S. 45
Varda, Robert 110
Veresayev, V.V. 52, 53, 64, 65, 74
Verne, Jules 9, 64
Wednesday Circle, The 27, 29, 43, 52, 60, 86, 98
Zaitsev, B.K. 50, 51
Zamiatin, Y.I. 71
Znaniye 42, 56, 68, 80, 85, 86, 104
Zolotoye Runo 85